Money's On The Dresser

Escorting, Porn and Promiscuity in Las Vegas

Christopher Daniels

Available through Ingram Press, and available for order through Ingram Press Catalogues

ISBN 978-1-62747-045-2

Dedication

This book is dedicated to clients and sex workers everywhere. Sex makes the world go 'round, so basically we are to thank for everything. You're welcome!

Acknowledgements

I think the best place to start is thanking all the men I have met as an escort. You are more than "clients" but I guess that's what I'll call you. Thank you for sharing your lives, your stories, a few days, an evening or just an hour with me. You've opened my eyes, you've shocked me, humbled me, pissed me off and helped shape me into the man I am today. I'm not quite sure if I fulfilled every fantasy you were looking for, but I am grateful to have met you all.

Now here's the list, in no particular order:

Thank you to Tom Bird for helping me bring my stories together and really figuring out what my book would be about. I came to you with seven chapters but still had no clue what the overall theme was. You listened to me, encouraged me and helped me piece together my story.

Thank you to Rama for all your help in getting this project finished and answering my endless amount of emails and questions.

Thank you to Derek and John Vairo Jr. for your help with the book cover and Mitchell Ivers for your encouragement, support and professional guidance.

Thank you to Mama Bear Scott for always opening your home to me and supporting me with my writing.

Thank you to SF Geek. Time with you is always enjoyable and I am thankful to have been with you during a new stage of your life after your partner passed away.

Thank you to OkieHomo. You're old, broke, peculiar and picky, but our times together were always a blast.

Thank you to Arpad Miklos. Not quite sure what I'm thanking you for, but I think of you often. I don't know what made you decide to do what you did, but I want you to know you are loved and missed. I looked up to you as an escort and performer and you truly are a legend.

Thank you to all my escort buddies. Going into this I thought you'd all be sketched out tweakers with an agenda to make money at any cost. Instead you became friends and brothers. I don't know if anyone can understand the bond we all share but I am grateful for it and for having all of you in my life. AJ (the original AJ), AJ Irons, David SF, Tristan Baldwin, Brayden, Ace, Christopher F, Vito and the list goes on. I am always here for you and I love you all.

I am happy to have had my book looked over by so many great people, one of whom is Mike Diamond. You always make me laugh and you constantly encourage me. Thank you for helping me figure out a name for this book. It literally took me a year to come up with hardly anything, but you came in with your dry wit and sarcasm and figured it out. You rock. I really do look up to you and can't wait until you are truly recognized for all of your talents. Unfortunately, you may need to die first because people really don't understand true talent until it's gone. I'M KIDDING! Come stay with me in Vegas. I'll pamper you and listen to you tell stories of the ballroom.

Thank you to Pokercomedy for going through my work and always taking the time to crack a few jokes (usually at my expense) and making me laugh.

Big thank you to Andrew Rosen. I appreciate your advice and for suggesting ways of being a better writer.

Thank you to Jesse in Las Vegas for your help. It was greatly appreciated and needed.

Thank you to Bj. You are a man of many words, which is why I love you, and you drive me crazy at times. You really did do me a huge service by going over my work and constantly encouraging me. You have opened your home to me and whenever we are together I have a great time. I loved shivering with you in your New York City apartment as we watched Raquel Welch and Bea Arthur variety specials. I love you buddy!

Thank you to CR for your help, encouragement and wonderful dinners. Sometimes you lectured me like a father figure and other times you listened. Either way, it meant a lot and I am glad to have you in my life.

Thank you to Wil for putting up with…everything. I don't know how you do it. I exhaust myself and you never seem to leave my life. You will always be family.

Thank you to Janell. If things were different, meaning if I were straight, we'd definitely be together right now. Thank you for always being my non-sexual blonde bombshell girlfriend and arm candy. Tell KC I say hi!

Thank you to DB for reading over my book and sharing your insight. You have been my number one fan for the past year and I love you.

Thank you to Lloyd for all your help and coming up with the tagline "Hemingway of Hooker". You always put a smile on my face.

Thank you so much to my webmaster Craig for always going above and beyond in helping me. I appreciate your work and your friendship.

Thank you to Dr Zellers. You are outstanding at your job and you have seen me through many stages of my life. Thank you for always laughing with me, listening and being supportive of me and what I do.

Thank you to Bobby. You also will always be family to me.

The list really could go on but I'll wrap it up. Thank you for reading and I hope you find a bit of yourself in these stories and you really do hear my voice.

Introduction

In 2006, everyone around me started reading and talking about the book "The Secret" by Rhonda Byrne. I decided to follow the crowd and read it myself. Within a few days I had finished the book and began making my vision board. As I brainstormed the list of things I wanted for myself, I decided one day I would write a book. I had no clue what I would write about, who would read it or how to go about publishing it, but I knew it would happen. I posted a photo of a book on my vision board and looked at it everyday.

Fast forward to 2009. My boyfriend of four years and I decided to go our separate ways. I needed money fast to get started on my own. I had heard about guys putting ads up online and working as escorts. I wasn't naive to what they were doing and it intrigued me. It sounded like something I wanted to try. After a year of working as an escort, friends kept telling me to write a book about my experiences, and after the events of Chapter One happened, I decided it was time to start writing. The stories came pouring out of me and I couldn't stop writing for about 8 months. I still had no clue what the book would be about, but I figured documenting the experiences I shared with some of the men in this book was a start. Here is my story.

Disclaimer

The statements and contents of this autobiographical work are true and are my interpretation of the truth. I have tried to recreate events, locales and conversations from my memories of them. Some names, places and identifying details have been changed to protect the privacy of individuals as well as their anonymity. Any time spent with another individual where any funds were exchange was simply for time spent only. Any sexual activity that is described in this autobiographical work was consensual. The author and publisher shall have no liability or responsibility to any person or entity regarding any loss or damage incurred, or alleged to have incurred, directly or indirectly, by the information contained in this book. My life experiences and views are my own that I am sharing with the general public. You, the reader, are responsible for your own choices, actions and results.

Chapter One

Ball Bashing and Incest

The phone rang around eleven on Sunday morning. It was August of 2011 and it was still boiling hot in Las Vegas. I was in my new king-size bed with both of my dogs by my side and a sheet barely covering my sweaty naked body. My comforter had fallen off the bed sometime during the night. I had a ceiling fan on full blast above me but it wasn't enough to cool me off and keep me away from the 110-degree desert heat outside. Most people would think of this as midday, but for me it was still early, especially after being out all night partying and drinking with friends. I hated keeping my phone on throughout the night, but if I didn't, I could end up missing out on too many clients.

I immediately recognized the 818 area code as being from Los Angeles. I figured it was just another rich Hollywood Hills or Beverly Hills guy in his fifties or sixties looking for an escort on his last day in town.

"Is this Christopher?" asked the man on the other end.

"Yes, it is. Who is this?" I asked, wondering what he was looking for. Nothing shocked me anymore, so I was mainly interested in him just putting his cards on the table.

"My name is Marvin. Have we talked before?" he asked.

I searched my memory for a Marvin in California. His voice seemed familiar, but I came up with nothing.

"I'm not too sure. What's going on, Marvin?" I asked curiously.

"I live in LA and I wanted to bring you out here for a few days of fun. Would you be interested in that?" He sounded like he had a definite plan of what this "fun" entailed, but his voice was not relaxed or inviting. Instead he sounded creepy. Right away, I began to think his request would be a little more fucked up than taking me out to dinner and seeing a show, or spending thirty to forty minutes in his room talking, a massage, and possibly more.

"Sure. How long did you want me to come out and stay with you?"

"Well, I was thinking three to five days, and I would pay you a thousand dollars a day to stay here with me in my home," he said with confidence.

"Okay, great," I replied. *A thousand dollars a day? Seriously?* This sounded too good to be true. I could have definitely used a few thousand dollars at that time! Generally, I don't like to do overnights with clients I don't know unless the money is really worth it, or if it gave me a chance to travel to a new place. I preferred sleeping in my own bed alone, so for me to do it a few days with a client in his bed had to be worth it.

"The only thing is, I have a few special requests," said Marvin.

Special requests? Oh God, that could mean anything from kissing, massage, or cuddling to water sports, bondage, or verbal and/or physical abuse.

"Okay... like what?" I asked, feeling less interested. Generally, "special requests" included things I was not always comfortable doing and required a lot of work and energy. I don't particularly like to cater to high-maintenance men with specific and elaborate sexual scenarios. I prefer men with more vanilla tastes who are looking for a boyfriend experience, like drinks, dinner, a show, talking, some light foreplay, and possibly more if they didn't cum just as the oral sex started.

"Well," Marvin continued, "I really get off on a guy kicking me in the balls. Is that something you could do?" He was now sounding like a dirty old man on the other end of the phone. This was obviously something he'd done before, and he was probably jerking off as he told me the details of what he got into. Shortly after I began escorting, I quickly noticed some of the men who called had no interest in hiring me. Rather, they would just call me with these elaborate sexual fantasies, and clearly they got off on telling them to me and hearing my voice on the other end.

This request sounded oddly familiar, but I wasn't sure if this was something I had been asked to do before or if this was just another odd fetish request. It was not something I had ever done, but as long as I wasn't getting kicked in the balls, I guess it was okay.

"Ummmmmm, okay," I responded. I still wasn't sure if I wanted to go through with this, but the money sounded good and maybe this was a chance to test my sexual limits. In this industry, I am constantly faced with opportunities to try new things sexually. Often I don't feel comfortable with what they want, but sometimes I like to explore new things and test my boundaries so I agree.

"How hard do you want me to kick you in the balls, and how often?" Five days of being kicked in the nuts sounded excessive, but who was I to judge?

"I want you to kick me as hard as you can in the balls whenever I tell you to do it. It'll probably be often and throughout the day. I'm serious, man. I want you to kick the shit out of my nuts and step on 'em. I want you to climb on top of me and jump on my dick like a trampoline."

I was confused. Was this guy serious? And why did this all sound so familiar?

"Okay, I guess I can do that," I said, feeling slightly sick to my stomach at the thought of all that physical pain done to someone's dick and balls. I remembered being an eight-year-old boy on the playground running across the field toward the jungle gym to play on the monkey bars. Some kids were playing soccer and accidentally kicked the ball off the field and it went flying toward me, smacking me right in the nuts. I felt shooting pains in my stomach, became very dizzy, and saw yellow stars just like in the cartoons. One of the kids ran over to me to get his ball and I handed it back to him even though I felt like I was about to pass out. He asked me if I was okay and I was barely able to get out the word "yep." The pain lasted a few hours and I would vividly feel it every time I saw someone on *America's Funniest Home Videos* get smacked in the groin. Maybe this wasn't for me, even though the money sounded amazing.

"And, on the last day of your visit, I will give you an extra fifteen hundred dollars for you to tie me down and kick me in the nuts until they are black and blue and I can't move anymore. I mean it, Chris... I want you to put big heavy, steel-toe army boots on and just kick the shit out of my dick."

All of a sudden, I remembered this conversation.

"What is your name again?" I asked.

3

"Marvin." As soon as he repeated his name, it all came back to me. I wasn't upset with his request, but I was pissed this guy wouldn't leave me the fuck alone and woke me up with his stupid fake sexual fantasy.

Marvin was someone who had called me a few times when I first began escorting two years ago. I had considered his odd requests because I thought he was serious, and if someone were going to pay me a few thousand dollars to kick him in the balls, then how could I say no to that much money? Money is money. Unfortunately, after his second and third phone call, I got the feeling this guy—like so many others—was only interested in wasting my time and giving me the run-around. A lot of these men who called with very specific requests were full of shit and had no intention of actually following through with me or any other escort.

"Listen, asshole," I said. "I think you're fucking gross. I don't give a shit with what you're into, but quit wasting my time, you twisted fuck, and leave me the fuck alone before I come out to LA, find you, and seriously bash the shit out of your balls!"

Before Marvin could respond, I hung up the phone. I remembered that he's well known to escorts, especially on the West Coast, for bothering guys with this odd-ball bashing requests and never actually hiring anyone. If that's what you get off on, fine, but don't wake me up on a Sunday morning just to waste my time with this shit.

I was still tired and needed to sleep off a few more vodka drinks from the night before. I had gone bar-hopping with my best friend Jonathan until five in the morning. All I remember was starting at a local gay country and western bar called Charlie's, moving to another bar called 8.5 and ending the night at Krave, the only gay nightclub on the Las Vegas Strip. When we got to Krave, we watched Shangela, one of the contestants from *RuPaul's Drag Race,* perform a Beyonce medley. Afterward, we took pictures with her, did shots, and told her how beautiful she was, something all drag queens love to hear from their adoring fans.

I tried to forget about the phone call and focus on breathing deeply until my body was completely relaxed. I was soon able to fall back asleep, only to be awakened again by my phone, this time from a blocked number. I rarely answered calls from blocked numbers because guys who called from blocked numbers were, like Marvin, generally not serious about hiring. Instead, they would waste my time with tons of questions about what I do and don't get into, and they would want to tell me their life story and play out some kind of elaborate fantasy they had with escorts.

It seemed like eighty-five to ninety-five percent of these men never actually hired escorts; instead, they were probably just jacking off on the other end of the phone, listening to an escort's voice. I pretty much stopped answering blocked calls soon after I began escorting, but that morning I was so sleepy I stupidly picked up.

"Hello?" I said, trying to sound awake and not hung over.

"Hi, is this Christopher Daniels?" asked the man on the other line.

"Yes, it is. Who is this?" I asked.

"My name is Tom, and I was wondering if you were free this afternoon." The man sounded normal, direct, and to the point. I was hoping there would be no beating around the bush and he wouldn't ask me a thousand questions. It made my life a lot easier when the clients knew what they wanted and were ready to set something up. It grated on my last nerve when they would ask me a million questions about height, weight, age, dick size, costs, what I will and will not do, fetishes, positions, if I was a top or a bottom, and so on. All of that information was clearly stated in my ads and there was no need to spend ten minutes asking questions.

"Yes, I am. What hotel are you staying at?" I asked.

"Mandalay Bay. I was wondering if you could come over to my hotel, fuck my son, and then fuck me."

I sat up, speechless. I paused and thought to myself, *Is this guy for real?* Immediately, I became suspicious yet slightly aroused. The idea of a hot father-and-son scenario turned me on, as long as the son was of legal age, but I had no clue if that was the kind of situation this man was talking about.

"How old is your son?" I asked.

"He's twelve and he's a virgin." Tom's voice didn't even flinch when he said this son. Suddenly, I began to feel ill and disgusted, just hearing the words come out of this man's mouth. Even though I knew

5

childhood sexual abuse is prevalent in both the gay and straight communities, it's not something I had experienced.

"Are you seriously asking me to have sex with your twelve-year-old son, and then have sex with you?" I asked incredulously.

There were so many things wrong with this request. I really began to worry. Was I talking to a cop working for some kind of sting operation, like *To Catch a Predator*? Was this a set-up? Were Chris Hanson and the *Dateline NBC* crew on the other line?

Unsure if he was full of shit or just fucking with me, I said, "Uhhhh... sir, I can't do that. That's, uh... I'm not sure if you understand, but you could get into a lot of trouble for something like that. So could I."

"Well, the thing is he wanted me to fuck him, and I was going to, but then we thought it would be fun to hire an escort, and he thinks you're really hot. All you have to do is fuck him as I watch you both, then you can fuck me and he'll watch us."

Even if the twelve-year-old wanted me to do this, it would still be sex with a minor. I felt guilty even hearing this man's request. This had to be a set-up; there was no way it was real. I thought I had stopped being shocked by requests since that one time a guy asked me to take a shit in his mouth—which apparently some guys really get into—but I guess this was a new one.

I wanted to scream at Tom and tell him how disgusting he was and how what he was doing was wrong on so many levels, but I couldn't because I was literally speechless. Finally I uttered, "I'm sorry, that's not something I can do."

"Okay, not a problem. We'll find someone else. Thanks." And Tom hung up.

One guy who wants me to kick the shit out of his balls and a father who wants me to fuck him and his twelve-year-old virgin son. All this is happening to me before noon on a Sunday. Welcome to my life.

Chapter Two

FAGGOT

Although I didn't come from a background most people would associate with someone in the sex industry, feelings I had are familiar to many who made similar choices. Even as a young kid, it was clear there was something missing in my life. My need for approval and love goes back as far as I can remember. I never felt like I fit in, whether at school, during recess or gym class, church, playing with the neighborhood boys, or at home. I always felt like I was standing on the outside of everything that was happening around me and never felt like I was a part of a community or group of people. The question of love was never an issue in my home, but I knew from a young age I wasn't anything like my older siblings or extended family. My family always loved me and was very proud of me and my accomplishments, but I always felt very distant from them and never felt like they fully understood what was going on in my mind.

Unfortunately, it always felt like something was keeping me from truly feeling close or connected to them. This caused me to become very withdrawn and shy in social settings, as well as apprehensive about putting myself out there or getting to know the people around me.

I didn't come from a broken home, I wasn't sexually abused, and I didn't even lose my virginity until I was nineteen. Aside from smoking pot, I didn't really start experimenting with drugs until my mid-twenties and, even then, only recreationally.

When I started escorting in 2009, I looked online for books, documentaries, interviews, movies, and TV shows about the world of male escorting. The only materials I could find were a few outdated books, magazine interviews, and YouTube video clips. They were anywhere from ten to twenty-plus years old. Most of the sources discussed male "hustlers" putting ads in the back pages of XXX magazines or standing on the street corner waiting to be picked up by middle-aged men throughout the night. Many of the accounts talked about these guys struggling with drug addiction, coming from broken homes, and living on the streets or in shitty hotel rooms. Most of them only escorted to support a drug habit. It all seemed very dark, sad, and depressing. I could relate to none of it, and I struggled to find current information on what it's like to work in the sex industry, because although it was all very new to me, I knew it couldn't be as bleak and dark as how people made it out to be.

I wasn't exposed to sex or pornography at a young age; I didn't even know how two men had sex until I was fourteen and a straight male friend explained it to me. Looking back, I am amused at how naive I was, especially considering how kids are so easily exposed to things like pornography and sex at younger and younger ages. It seems like most fourteen- and fifteen-year-olds today have more knowledge and experience than I did in my late teens and early twenties. (This isn't making me sound like a very interesting escort, is it?)

I don't speak for everyone in the sex industry, but in my experience, I have come to learn that not all escorts and porn stars are meth-head, drug-abusing sex addicts who will give a ten-dollar blow-job to buy their next hit.

During my first week as a male escort, I got a phone call from a Las Vegas native. His name was Kyle, a man in his early sixties. He invited me to spend the evening with him and two other escorts visiting from Los Angeles. Their names were Christopher and Kristofer. I wasn't sure how he was going to keep the three of us all straight, but I agreed to meet them the following evening. When I got to the hotel room, I expected to walk into the room to see some trashy, shirtless, drunk young men smoking cigarettes and high on something. Instead, I walked into a room where I met Kyle and two good-looking men in their early thirties. Christopher Number One was a massage therapist from Los Angeles, and Kristofer Number Two was an actor from North Hollywood. Both were clean-cut, good-looking men who looked like the boy-next-door type. Neither did porn, had ever touched drugs, or even drank much. In fact, Kristofer admitted his biggest weakness was penny slot machines and Mountain Dew soda. These two guys were not what I had expected of the majority of male escorts.

We spend two or three hours that night talking and getting to know each other before finally moving to the bedroom to do what we ultimately came to do. Kyle was a nice man and really got off on spending quality time going to dinner, shows, hanging out and talking with male escorts. He enjoyed getting to know us, giving us advice and listening to the things we were going through in our personal lives. Sexual contact had very little to do with our meetings, but eventually it happened. Christopher, Kristofer, Kyle, and I moved to the bedroom to get things started. Kyle took out some Vaseline to jerk one of us off and make out while the other two would fuck like animals. All three of us appeared to be such nice, clean-cut, well-mannered men, but once the clothes came off and the lights went down, Christopher and Kristofer became aggressive dominating tag-team tops and took turns fucking me. I remember thinking halfway through the orgy, "How could this be considered work?" I was having a blast, and Kyle was getting off on just sitting back and watching us go at it.

I read many accounts of guys and girls who went into the sex industry, and most came from broken homes or struggled with addictions and abuse. I, on the other hand, spent my childhood going to church up to three times a week, twice on Sunday and Bible study on Wednesday. I took part in acting, dance, and music lessons my whole life. I listened to children's Bible story tapes produced by *Focus on the Family* every night, and I would spend hours singing along to Broadway as a kid. *Annie* was my favorite musical, and I could rock out the opening song "Maybe" better than any girl under the age of ten auditioning for the show.

Everything I did as a child was pretty much considered "gay" by my peers, classmates, teachers, and family members. I was the typical gay kid in school. I spent my childhood in school musicals and ballet class and begged my mom to put me in cooking and sewing lessons. It still makes me laugh when I told my mom I was gay at age twenty-two and she had a hard time dealing with it. She's the one who went along with putting me in cooking, sewing, knitting, dance, and violin lessons, after weeks or even months of me pleading and begging her. Other than becoming gay, how else would I have turned out? I was the youngest of five kids and my three older brothers were always the more athletic ones. I remember spending a lot of time in hockey arenas, watching my brothers play on various church and local hockey teams. I pretty much detested all sports but enjoyed going to their games for the eye candy. Two of my brothers went to the same Bible College. I'd love to go spend the day with them because their friends would always be hanging around and sometimes shirtless and I thought they were so fucking hot. I fantasized about their friends all the time and I'd get instant erections watching them walk around topless and freeballing in gym shorts.

As a child, I didn't completely understand what "gay" meant. I knew I enjoyed looking at attractive men and I remember falling in love with guys or having crushes at least once a week. I had no clue why, but I knew it raised a few eyebrows when my sibling's friends came over and saw me playing with dolls, dressing up, or playing house in the basement. My parents never encouraged me to play with girl's toys, but they knew it was what I liked and I don't think they knew quite how to handle it, so they just loved me and tried their best to make me content. I have to give credit to them because not every parent would react so graciously if they had a son as effeminate or as vocal about wanting to do everything my female schoolmates did.

Before I came out of the closet to my family, friends would laugh at me when I told them my parents didn't know I was gay. They would look at me as if to say, "How could they not know? Look at yourself." It wasn't meant as an insult or mean-spirited, and I understood where they were coming from, but I honestly believe my family was pretty naive and really had no understanding of what being gay was, or even what gay men were really like. They knew I was different and loved me for that. For that I am forever grateful. Telling them was still difficult even if all signs pointed to G-A-Y. They couldn't fully be okay with it because from what they knew, and from what the Bible taught, homosexuality was wrong and there was no way around it. To my family, the Bible was the word of God, and that was that.

When I was struggling about whether or not to tell my family I was gay, my friends would often ask, "But doesn't your family want you to be happy? If being gay is who you are and makes you happy, isn't it all that matters?" I would think, *Not to my family,* but would simply tell them, "I guess so." For many Christians, happiness is not the most important thing in life. Holiness and following God's word are more important. Therefore if you are not happy, it is something you need to pray about. Growing up, I was taught that your personal relationship with Jesus Christ was all that mattered, and you needed to do whatever it took to work on that relationship according to the Bible. Everything else was secondary. Your happiness was not an issue you focused a lot of attention on.

I was taught by my family and church that even if you had to bear burdens, such as an addiction or sexual dysfunction (like they thought homosexuality was) here on earth, it would be okay as long as you suppressed the urges. The struggle and pain would all be worth it when you reached heaven. With this mindset, I grew up thinking being both gay and happy wasn't an option. I would have to be holy and miserable to get into heaven and bear my cross of homosexuality. Sounds like fun, doesn't it?

I grew up in Regina, Saskatchewan, Canada, and there was—and still is—very little gay culture. In my family, I don't remember having a television during the first years of my life, and when we finally got one, it was black and white and only had three local television stations. We really had no clue about what was going on around us as far as pop culture, and I had no idea about the growing gay culture of the '80s and '90s.

For my family there was church, school, and a lot of books for learning. The dinner table was where the majority of the conversations took place every night. When I was five or six years old my sister, in high school at the time, was reading about a new disease called HIV/AIDS and told us that most of the people being infected were gay or drug users. One of my brothers—as well as myself—didn't know what being gay meant and when we asked, my sister told us, without being too graphic, that being gay was when two men had sex with each other.

From that simple description, I realized I must be gay. Even at that young age, I knew I had a deep connection with men and a desire to be with them. I didn't know what sex was, but I knew I was attracted to other boys my age, as well as older men, so I figured it all meant the same thing. I must be gay. Jumbling the facts, I figured that if I was gay, I would inevitably contract HIV/AIDS and die like the men described in my sister's book. I felt like the overall tone of the book was that gay men and drug users deserved to get HIV/AIDS because what they were doing was immoral and wrong. It wasn't rational, but I was young and had no real understanding of what being gay really meant. Instead, I gathered from my family's reaction that being gay was dirty and disgusting; that these gay men were vile individuals. At that moment I decided I should definitely keep my mouth shut about the neighborhood boys I had a crushes on and try my best to hide these feelings.

From a very young age, I felt like my fate was sealed. I was gay, would be rejected by my family, die a slow horrible death of pneumonia, lying in dirty diapers as I shit myself in a hospital bed somewhere surrounded by people wearing face masks and hospital gowns afraid to touch me. Every time I remembered hearing my sister talk about the disease, I immediately experienced a sense of loneliness. From that point on, I felt an immense sense of rejection and isolation from everyone around me, because my family wanted nothing to do with gay people, and I was sure I had this sickness called homosexuality.

I remember a few years later we were all sitting at the dinner table and there had been a news story about gay men on television. My mom made it very clear that "I could handle it if one of you had a child out of wedlock but I don't know what I would ever do if one of you told me you were gay" and shook her head in disgust.

Even though I did not have a clear understanding of the complexities of being gay, I knew I was. If not, why did I want to kiss boys so badly and not girls? But I learned at a young age to quickly bury that feeling deep down inside. There was no way I was going to let anyone find out, and I would go to great lengths to hide it not only from others, but even to myself. It would be years before I would be able to finally admit to myself I was gay, and even more years before I would be comfortable with it.

It was clear that I was not like other boys. For my whole childhood, people would question who I was and the activities I took part in. I was taunted and ridiculed daily by my classmates and often went home crying. As a young boy and a teenager growing up in a prairie town in Saskatchewan, I would be called names, people would jokingly ask if I was a girl, and I would be the butt of many jokes. I can remember on a daily basis someone would call me a faggot, a homo, sissy or a fairy. This created a lot of social anxiety in me and I would be petrified walking into an unknown situation such as a birthday party, a school or church event, or the beginning of a new school year. You'd think church would be a safe and loving place, but I remember attending church events and kids would laugh at me because I looked and acted effeminately and I was a lot more sensitive than most other boys. In the eighth grade my mother, school councilor, and I decided enough was enough and I needed to change schools. The teasing, loneliness, depression, and tears had become too much, and it seemed like the only option. Within my first thirty minutes at my new school, a fellow classmate had walked over to me, asked me if I was a faggot, and before I could even answer, he grabbed me, put me in a head lock, and choked me, and I nearly passed out. I didn't understand what was happening. It was almost as if I had the words GAY and PLEASE BEAT ME UP tattooed on my forehead. Nobody in the new school had even said two words to me, but I guess everyone could tell there was something off about the new kid and decided to make me their new punching bag. To this day, the anxiety created is something I struggle with. People have often told me that when they first met me they thought I was bitchy and standoffish; I wouldn't describe myself that way, but the truth is I can be aloof and distant. I'm not trying to make excuses, but I think this all comes from the social anxiety I had when I was a kid.

As I grew older, the crying from all the teasing stopped because shame set in about showing emotion. In my mind, crying was a sign of weakness. Weak men were effeminate, and effeminate men were gay. Any signs of weakness seemed to attract more negative attention from school bullies and neighborhood boys who would walk by and call me "faggot" on a daily basis. It was obvious to everyone I was effeminate, but I vehemently denied being gay and refused to accept the label.

Trying desperately not to attract attention from peers my own age, I was also trying to avoid any odd looks or suspicion from people in the church and even my family. Nobody seemed to have any understanding of homosexuality. For them, it was simple: Gay men had sex with other men, and men who had sex with other men usually contracted AIDS, died, and went to hell. All of this negativity caused me to close off more

13

and more, and my sadness as a young kid turned into a very dark, deep depression by the time I was a teenager. I started to become incredibly angry at the world, and there was a never-ending sense of sadness and gloom in my life that I could not resolve. I hated who I was, and I hated the same sex feelings I wrestled with daily. Sometimes, when I reread my journals from my childhood, I see a hurt, sad, angry, wounded kid crying out from the pages. I was petrified of death because I wasn't sure if I would get into heaven if I died because I constantly struggled with same-sex feelings. I knew I was gay, but I wished for death almost every single day to end these feelings of sadness. I would think about how amazing it would feel to be taken from this world in my sleep, and pray there was a way to die without feeling pain or having to do it myself. The depression I felt was all I knew then, and looking back, it is devastating to think that such a young kid constantly fantasized about a way out of this world.

I had always loved to perform and take part in theater groups, but it wasn't until the summer after I turned thirteen that things began to change. I went to a Shakespeare camp, where we studied and performed *As You Like It*. At camp I met great kids my age—some still friends—and we spent four weeks together memorizing the play, building sets for it, and costuming the show. It was here that I finally found out what gay sex was. I hadn't realized being gay involved more than boy crushes, kissing, pressing your body up against another boy, or maybe even putting your dicks in each other's mouths. To me, gay sex was all about kissing and holding each other and feeling emotionally connected to another guy. That was all I wanted, so I figured that was all there was. I guess I didn't hear anyone mention anything about getting HIV/AIDS from having unprotected anal sex and cumming inside someone's ass.

That summer at the Shakespeare theater camp, my friend LeeAnder and I were in the wardrobe room designing costumes. We were all given the name of someone else in the play whose costume we had to design. Mine was for a girl named Rita, and we all spent every afternoon working on our partners' costumes, and the construction of the sets. While working and designing our costumes, we were all talking about Tracey, the head of wardrobe, because he was clearly gay and we thought that was the weirdest and coolest thing ever. Making fun of him was my way of diverting any eyes from me and directing it toward the guy who was so clearly a raging homosexual. Regardless of the fact that we were in a theater camp, we were eleven- to fourteen-year-old kids, and the whole concept of being gay made us all giggle. It made me squirm because I knew I was just as much a "queen" as Tracey. When talking with LeeAnder, I said, "I don't even understand how they do it. Like how do two guys even have sex?" I asked this jokingly, but I was actually serious. I really didn't know what sex was, outside of kissing and a few other things.

LeeAnder, who was straight, just looked at me in disbelief and said, "Are you serious?"

I just stared blankly at him. I guess he thought of all people I should know what gay sex was, but I honestly had no clue.

"Gay guys have sex by putting their dicks in each other's assholes," he said matter-of-factly.

His news rocked my world, and gay sex finally made sense. After that discussion with LeeAnder, along with my teenage hormones, I became hornier and very curious about what gay guys were actually doing in bed. Like most twelve- to thirteen-year-old boys, I became obsessed with sex even if I wasn't quite sure how it all worked.

The summer theater program had been the best experience of my life so far, and I nearly had an emotional breakdown when it came to an end. I met so many wonderful people and we became best friends over the four weeks we spent together. We were all theater kids, and to some extent, most of us were a little different than our school peers. I'm not sure if any of the other kids struggled with their sexuality quite like I did and, to be honest, I think I was the only one who was actually gay. We were just boys and girls from different backgrounds who loved theater and felt that special bond. For once, it was fun to fit in and to belong.

A year after my summer doing *As You Like It,* I began ninth grade at a high school called Sheldon-Williams Collegiate. The majority of my high school years were spent hanging out with various groups of people who were all involved in theater, dance, and music in some way. I began to meet guys who identified themselves as gay, and a few girls who were open about having had sexual experiences with other girls. This was a select group of people who were incredibly open-minded and very honest about their sexuality. I continued to repress my gay feelings because I knew my family, church, and most schoolmates would not accept it. But I was unable to fully hold back my feelings. I think all my friends were tired of asking if I was gay because I would deny it or shy away from the answer, so instead they just left me alone to work it out on my own. I'm sure they figured it was just a matter of time until I came out.

It wasn't until my freshmen year in high school that I saw two men having sex, and this nearly made my head and my dick spontaneously combust from excitement. My friends at school were kind of like band or show choir geeks, but a lot cooler. They were so "above" everyone and confident in themselves. I wanted to be like them, and they definitely helped shape my teenage years. One night, I was at my friend Jennifer's house with another girl named Jenna-Lynn. They both wanted to show me *The Rocky Horror Picture Show*. All my older friends were obsessed with the movie and knew all the lyrics and choreography to the musical numbers. When we watched the scene of Frank-N-Furter molesting Brad, I was blown away and nearly came in my pants. When the movie was done, I told my friends that it had been the first time I had seen two guys together.

"Really?" asked Jennifer. "That's nothing! Here, I'm going to show you gay porn. I stole a video from this weird couple who I babysit for." Jennifer was a seemingly well-behaved girl, and everyone's parents loved her, but she had a naughty streak. She would shoplift, buy me alcohol and cigarettes, and make out with girls when she got drunk at parties. She was incredibly open about her sexuality, and we spent hours talking about sex and all the things she had done with guys and girls. During my freshman year, she would take me driving in her 1986 Chevette, and we would skip school and chain-smoke menthol cigarettes while singing along to Donny Osmond in *Joseph and the Amazing Technicolor Dreamcoat*. We were badass show-choir kids. She would steal porn from that one couple, as well as raid her brother's porn stash. I always knew she had some porn in her bedroom, but I had no idea porn with two guys even existed. She brought out a VHS tape called *Bi Bi American Style* and fast-forwarded to the scene with two guys. The video was awful, the actors were from the early eighties and not very attractive, but I didn't care. I was watching dicks go into asses and men kissing, sucking dicks, and eating cum. I literally thought I was going to have a heart attack from watching my first guy-on-guy sex scene. From that point on I finally knew what gay sex was all about. And I was hooked.

My sexual experiences were pretty limited during high school. At fourteen, a friend of mine spent the night after a cast party for a musical we were doing. He slept on my floor, and throughout the course of the night we talked about everything. We discussed school, sex, our families, the churches we belonged to and much more. After a few hours, I got the impression he wanted me to lie next to him, so I joined him on the floor. We had been drinking, and it got flirtatious between us as the night wore on. It took me an hour of inching toward him to finally touch him. When I finally cuddled up close to him, he didn't do anything. It took another hour for my hand to make its way down his body and touch his dick before he pushed me off. I crawled back to bed, humiliated. I thought I had hit the jackpot, potentially finding another guy who was like me, but I was wrong and felt like a complete fool. I'm not sure if he struggled with being gay or if he had wanted something more to happen, but within a few months the entire school knew what I had done and I was devastated. I went from finally feeling somewhat sexually liberated within my group of friends and accepted at school to feeling ashamed, rejected, and the butt of many jokes for the rest of my high school years. Throughout the next few years, every time anything sexual happened between a classmate and me, it would usually end up with the other guy getting freaked out and hating me. I think they would feel shame, confusion, and guilt about what we did, and they didn't know how to process those emotions. They'd usually end up making fun of me with everyone else, turning away from me, never looking me in the eyes again. Eventually, the name-calling would start, and the guy I had experienced a few moments of intimacy with would be with everyone else whispering faggot, homo, queer, pansy, and so on. There were a few times guys would spit on me and laugh. I had no idea what to do but keep walking and act as if nothing happened. It took a long time before I was able to let myself open up to others sexually and emotionally because of this, and for years, I would expect any guy I was with to eventually turn on me.

After my sophomore year, my older friends graduated and I was left with very few friends my own age. Things got worse and worse between my classmates and me, and the teasing got me so down I would skip at least one class every other day. Again, I thought maybe the solution was to transfer schools, and I somehow managed to talk my parents into it. My family had moved and I started classes at a school down the street from my house called Balfour Collegiate. From day one at Balfour, I worked incredibly hard not to speak to anyone, say anything during class, or talk to any teachers or do anything that would put me in a spotlight, except for joining show choir... a boy's gotta sing, right? I completely changed the way I dressed, wearing only boring, drab solid-colored clothes. Almost everything I wore was army green or denim. It didn't really work, though, and by the time my senior year came around I was the butt of many jokes as "the gay kid"... again! I literally stayed silent in almost every class, but the kids still saw me as a target for teasing. I would go home hurt, angry, and depressed, but I would often jerk off thinking about the guys who had ridiculed me. They were always the hot jock and popular type who I hated, yet I desperately wanted to be loved and accepted by them at the same time. Talk about self loathing homosexual, right?

At Balfour, my depression worsened, and although I was fully aware of the physical changes taking place in my body, especially my increasing sex drive, the thing I wanted most was for a guy to love and be affectionate with and who would accept me. I wanted to have sex and be sexually free, but I was more interested in an emotional connection with another guy, and neither seemed to be happening. As my depression worsened, my self-hatred grew. I hated the fact that nothing seemed to be working the way I wanted, and the only way I could escape the pain was to imagine the day I would leave home, leave the small-mindedness of Regina, and run away to a place where I could be a part of a gay community, go to gay bars, and do all those "vile" things my family and church warned me about. I remember hearing sermons and reading articles in *Focus on the Family* magazine on what the gay lifestyle was really about. They painted it out to be a life of drug-induced parties, orgies, and gay pride marches in leather harnesses waving rainbow flags. I fantasized about a day when I could be a part of all the debauchery and sin they warned me about and finally fit in. And so began my seemingly never-ending countdown until the days I would leave home and start a new life—a "gay" life.

Chapter Three

From Prairie Boy to Las Vegas Show Boy

For a year after high school, I stayed in Regina to continue studying ballet at the Royal Conservatory of Music and Dance. I was focused on becoming a professional dancer and was learning ballet, modern, and jazz anywhere from four to eight hours a day and sometimes seven days a week. I earned and saved money working at a shoe store and at a children's daycare. Eventually I began looking at ballet schools in the United States where I could study dance and begin a new life. At nineteen years old, I was accepted to a ballet school in Torrington, Connecticut, called the Nutmeg Conservatory. I continued to work hard that year to save money and refine my ballet and modern dance technique. I would usually work up to forty hours a week and study dance in the evenings and on weekends. I wasn't completely sold on moving to Torrington, but I knew it had to be better than Regina, and I pressed forward to get the hell out of Saskatchewan.

I packed up my things in June 2000 to move to Torrington for the Nutmeg Ballet's Summer Intensive Dance Program. Torrington was not anything like I was hoping for. I had expected to live in a place that would have the energy of a big city and maybe a little gay culture. Instead, it looked like an old factory town that had absolutely no life in it. It was dreary, buildings were falling apart, and there was absolutely no nightlife or culture. To make the best of it, I told myself at least I was only an hour or so from New York City, and that anything was better than Regina, Saskatchewan.

That summer, things at the Nutmeg Conservatory didn't quite work out as planned. One of the male teachers thought my talents would be better suited to dancing in the corps de ballet, similar to a chorus position in a musical, and he recommended I work with a professional ballet company in Oklahoma City. At the end of the summer, I packed up again, this time for Oklahoma City, another shitty city, but less shitty than Torrington, so I didn't care. I was excited to be out on my own, away from the gloomy cold weather of the Saskatchewan prairies.

I ended up spending two years in Oklahoma City dancing for a small company called Ballet Oklahoma, which had about fifteen dancers. I spent a lot of time on my own, falling in and out of depression due to loneliness and boredom. Most of the other dancers in the company were older than I was, and it was difficult making a connection with anyone. I hoped my first year away from home would be similar to the college experience of parties, dating people my own age, drunken hook-ups, and debauchery, but it wasn't. It was a quiet life of dancing five days a week and nothing too exciting on the weekends. I didn't own a car that first year in Oklahoma City, leaving me to depend on my roommate, Tori, and the few friends I made in the company for rides. Tori was a nice Connecticut girl I had met at the Nutmeg Conservatory. She and I started at Ballet Oklahoma at the same time and decided to live together in a two-bedroom apartment on Meridian Avenue in Oklahoma City.

As far as dating and sex, my first year in Oklahoma was unspectacular. I dated a few guys and spent a lot of time online chatting on websites like gay.com or in the chat rooms on AOL and Yahoo, which were very popular at the time. That is what gay men were doing in 2000 and 2001. I was only nineteen, and couldn't get into the bars, so I'd go in chat rooms, meet guys there, talk on the phone, and meet up in person if we were interested in each other. I dated a few guys, but nothing too serious or memorable. Now not only was I bored and lonely, but incredibly sexually frustrated and horny.

After my first contract with the ballet company expired in the summer of 2001, I got a job dancing at a theater called Discoveryland USA to perform in the musicals *Oklahoma* and *Seven Brides for Seven Brothers.* I moved to Tulsa, Oklahoma, since the theater was located nearby in a small town called Sand Springs. Soon after that, I met a guy named Mason and started dating him.

Mason was struggling with alcohol and drug addictions, so I resisted dating him initially. Eventually I gave in because the sex was too good and what else was I supposed to do? I was living in Tulsa, doing a musical in the middle of nowhere. He drove me crazy from the moment we started hanging out. Although I had never met an alcoholic or drug user, it was clear there was something wrong with this kid. He would constantly get excessively drunk or go on crystal meth binges and not sleep for days, so we had an emotional turbulent relationship from the beginning.

Despite our rocky relationship, Mason and I spent the summer drinking Natural Ice beer and Captain Morgan's Spiced Rum and smoking a lot of weed. We were both underage so we had to sneak into gay bars. It was a fun time, but there was nothing substantial in the relationship. We were both young, Mason was dealing with his demons, and I was searching for someone to take care of me and of course have sex with on a regular basis. These issues, along with codependency, was not helpful for either one of us. At the end of the summer, I went back to dance in Oklahoma City, and Mason's parents shipped him off to rehab in Texas.

I went back to Ballet Oklahoma in the fall to continue dancing. But my time in the company came to an abrupt end the following spring when I was let go from the company. I was asked to leave because the director sensed I did not want to be there, and he was right. My heart just wasn't in it. I was miserable in Oklahoma City, still dealing with my sexuality and becoming a gay man. The other dancers were nice, but instead of feeling a part of the company, I felt completely alone. I was a twenty-year-old boy ready to explode out of the closet, but I had no idea how to do it. I still wasn't even sure if being gay was acceptable and would continuously deal with the guilt and shame that had been eating away at me for so many years.

Nine months before I was let go from Ballet Oklahoma, the world watched as planes flew into the World Trade Center, the Pentagon, and a field in Pennsylvania, I—along with the rest of the world—was confused and unsure what to make of it. The terrorist attacks caused a lot of stress and more depression and grief in me, and I didn't know how to make sense of it all. I was in desperate need of comfort and human consolation. I had not made peace with my homosexuality, so I turned to the only other thing I knew, which was the Christianity I grew up with. After much research and prayer, I ran into the arms of an ex-gay ministry called First Stone Ministries in Oklahoma City. It "helped" people overcome same sex desires as well as other "sexual dysfunctions."

I attended weekly counseling sessions and group meetings at First Stone Ministries—a well-known ex-gay organization—similar to the international ex gay ministry Exodus International. Along with private and group counseling sessions, we were encouraged to attend group outings where we "affirmed ourselves as men." We would do things like fish; have barbecues, play softball, and participate in Bible studies, praise and worship services, and prayer circles. We would affirm each other as men and pray to God to remove our same-sex desires and heal our sexual deviancies as we desperately tried to reconcile our broken emotional and sexual pasts.

Some of the men in the groups struggled with other sexual dysfunctions that were not just limited to homosexuality. These men dealt with issues such as childhood sexual abuse, rape, pornography addictions. Some were child molesters, and one guy had had sex with animals on his farm growing up in Oklahoma. Some were just plain old sex addicts and chronic masturbators—the tamest of the bunch—and we all hung out together, praying to God to take away the gay, bisexuality, porn-addiction, or animal-fucking urges. We were told to steer clear of masturbation, of gay men and women, and of anything from our past that would remind us of the life we were trying to leave. We were pressured to purge our homes of any books, music, movies, magazines, and pictures that had homosexual content or reminded us of the sinful life we were fighting to leave behind. I wanted to do what I thought God wanted me to do, so I jumped in fully and became an active member. I threw away countless CDs, books, movies, pictures, and any clothes that might have been perceived as gay.

We were also instructed to "pray about" and discard any items in our home that reminded us of our past homosexual lifestyle. These could be anything: a bedspread, a decorative pillow you bought with an ex-partner, pictures of you and gay friends, gifts from gay friends, etc. After numerous cleansings of my apartment, I had barely anything left, but I guess it was what God wanted, so I felt pressured to listen and obey.

A majority of the ministry was donation and volunteer-based; it depended on its members to help out. Every week I stuffed envelopes, answered phones and even painted rooms and moved furniture during an office "redecoration."

The summers in Oklahoma were very hot, so one day I decided to wear a tank top and white linen pants for comfort. The First Stone Ministries office was in the basement of an office building, and sometimes the air-conditioning didn't work very well. I wasn't about to spend the whole day sweating as I stuffed envelopes with letters asking for donations, so I put on the most comfortable things I owned. When I went to the office on that July day to help with some filing and other tasks, I was pulled aside by Sylvester, the director of the ministry, and told the way I dressed was too suggestive and it might be distracting to the men struggling with same-sex desires. I had worn this outfit numerous times before and immediately I thought, *But it's so hot in here... I'm here working for free and you're reprimanding me for the way I'm dressed?* I was embarrassed and felt like the slutty high school girl who gets sent to the principal for wearing a crop top and short-shorts, smacking her bubble gum, and twirling her hair. I did as I was told and threw out the tank top and pants as soon as I got home. I was frustrated because I was trying to do anything and everything to heal myself of homosexuality but yet again I failed. I was also upset because I had to throw away one of my favorite and most comfortable summer outfits, but I figured it's what Jesus would have wanted.

I want to commend the people at ex-gay ministries for trying to help people, but their efforts are based on the misinformation and misinterpreted Bible they believed in. The reality is that ministries like First Stone are clearly a joke, filled with people desperately trying to affirm their own decisions to leave their "wicked ways" and live a holy life of servitude to God. Nobody leading these ministries is an actual doctor or licensed therapist, and the only thing they are doing is screwing up future generations of confused people who could make use of an educated mental health specialist. They were not going to find that at an ex-gay ministry.

In the weekly support group, one man "struggled with pornography." From what he told us, his wife of seventeen years found him reading pornographic magazines—*Playboy*—and after several incidences of finding his "stash" she kicked him out of the house they had with their five kids. Now he was living with his mother and sleeping on her couch. Even as I was going through ex-gay therapy and followed the teachings of First Stone Ministries, I remember seeing this man weeping and crying out to God, begging for forgiveness, and I thought, *Really? All this drama for reading* Playboy*? She kicked her husband out for that?* This situation confused me, and it caused some doubt to enter my mind as to whether or not this was really the path I should be taking. The men, their families, and their churches were a strange bunch, but I still felt convinced it was where I needed to be. I also continued to spend every evening on my knees—literally—praying to God to "take the gay away."

After being let go from the ballet company in Oklahoma City, I got accepted to a Christian ballet school in Jackson, Mississippi. I was at a crossroad where I didn't know what the next step in my life was, but I took a chance and moved to dance in the apprentice program of the Christian Ballet Company. Working with the ballet company and living in Jackson was probably one of the most unpleasant times I have ever gone through. Being there was like stepping back to an era where black people still sat in the back of the bus. There wasn't even a local chapter of an ex-gay ministry, because being gay there was kept so deeply in the closet, people hadn't even come out to be told to go back in by their church leaders.

The ballet school and company were just as much of a joke as the rest of my experience in Jackson. I was reprimanded weekly for wearing my ballet tights too tight in the crotch area, and I was forced to wear baggy shorts over my tights so I would not offend anyone. I was also told my body language—the way I danced, spoke, and acted in and out of rehearsals—was too effeminate. This was something the pastoral leader of the company told me I needed to work on and he threatened to ban me from touring with the company if I didn't change my body language, the way I carried myself in front of others and my style of dancing. He also told me I couldn't live with another male in the school because others would assume we were gay and having some type of sexual relationship with each other. The list went on and on, and I felt like I was going crazy there. After four months, I left the school without a single regret. This ballet company in Jackson still exists and continues to groom future generations of young dancers to be homophobic while converting sinners to the teachings of Jesus Christ through dance.

I hung around Jackson for another five months, doing short-term gigs with a few other companies in Illinois and Nashville before giving up, realizing I had to get the hell out of Jackson to create a life for myself. My ballet career was going nowhere and I was not suited for the life of a company dancer. The money was not great, and it was not what I wanted for myself artistically or personally. I wanted to perform in shows that would use my training in musical theater and jazz dancing.

I decided to audition for several production companies specializing in hiring dancers for production shows on cruise ships. In the span of a week, Royal Caribbean Productions received my audition video, hired me, and flew me out to Hollywood, Florida, to begin rehearsals and start a new life on the seven seas on one of their ships, the *Nordic Empress.*

I would go on to spend about two and a half years traveling and performing on cruise ships. I was able to see many parts of the world and meet some amazing people. Ship life is special, completely unique, and unlike anything else I had ever experienced.

I am grateful for my time on ships, but it is not something I would repeat. There is little to no gay life, and fraternizing with passengers is grounds for immediate dismissal. I would often fuck less-than-desirable crew members—guys and occasionally girls—out of sheer desperation and because I would be doing seven-, eight-, and sometimes nine-month contracts on ships. My options for dating and sex were at times, limited, so I would have to make do with what I was given. Even though sleeping with passengers was strictly forbidden, and I did see several crew members (some of whom were good friends) dismissed immediately after they were caught and sometimes escorted off the ship at random ports in Third World countries in the Caribbean, I didn't really care. I took chances, managing to hook up with passengers a few times during each contract, taking the walk of shame back to my cabin early in the morning.

On my second ship contract, another male dancer in the show named DJ talked me into going to a bathhouse with him, and this started my obsession with them. We would port in Vancouver every Saturday, and I spent each time there from 10 a.m. to 5 p.m. at the local bathhouse on Davie Street, fucking and getting fucked by guys. I'd fuck, get fucked, and finger, fist, and suck anything. I had so much pent-up sexual aggression built up, I couldn't fight it anymore. I had only a few short-term boyfriends and sexual experiences by this time, and I felt like I needed to catch up. I was tired and frustrated with all the ex-gay-Christian bullshit I was telling myself to believe, so I gave into what my body wanted. I was a total slut and a natural-born cocksucker, and I loved it. I didn't care if I went to hell. I just wanted to go to the bathouse, fuck, and feel good. I had sex with nearly anything that moved in the bathhouse. I would fuck or suck as many guys I could find in one day because I needed to get out all this sexual frustration from being on a ship all week. There were times I was so desperate and horny on board, I began having sex with a few girls. It wasn't something I would do regularly, but I had a loyal group of girls who liked to play around. The sex was nice, but it sort of felt like throwing a hot dog down a hallway. It was not something I did on a regular basis if I could help it.

I was in my early twenties and I had been away from home for a few years. I was coming to terms with the fact that I was gay, but I still struggled with the issue of my "salvation." It took years before I would finally be okay with being a gay man who was not destined for hell because of it. A lot of the old demons still creep up now and then, and I do battle them but it's nowhere nearly as bad as it once was. When I'm having the time of my life partying, dancing, drinking, or having sex with a beautiful man, a tiny voice will sneak into my head and say, "You realize you're going to hell for this, right?" I overcome them with a little bit of cognitive behavior therapy or the recitation of a few personal affirmations my therapist taught me like:

"You are a good man, Christopher."

"You are perfect the way you are."

"It's okay to be gay."

"There is nothing wrong with who you are."

These affirmations are simple and basic, but I still need a reminder every now and then. Undoing years of being told the way you are is wrong, sinful, abnormal, and an abomination is an ongoing process I continue daily.

In 2004, I was working on the *Golden Princess* cruise ship sailing throughout the Caribbean. After four months, we went to New York City and then to Europe to cruise the British Isles. This is when I met Patrick, in May 2004. I'm not sure what it was about him, but I thought he was cute and we got along well. We started dating soon after we met and it was nice. This was my first real relationship and I jumped into it head on. I was ready to settle down and get married after a few weeks, and he felt the same about me. A big part of me wanted to be with Patrick for the sake of being with someone. I enjoyed being with him and he always knew how to make me feel special; I grew to love him and we decided the following January to leave the cruise ship and start a new life in Las Vegas. Patrick was from there, so it seemed like an easy transition for us. I had heard there was steady dance work there, and it seemed natural for a dancer to go from dancing on a cruise ship to the Las Vegas strip.

The move was not easy and tested our relationship numerous times. It took a while before Patrick started his job as a casino dealer and even longer before I landed my first dancing gig on the strip. Eventually, Patrick landed a job working as a dealer at the MGM Grand. I got a job dancing in the long-running show *Jubilee* at Bally's Hotel. We had a good life living in Vegas, going to work at our casinos and socializing with friends whenever we had time off.

Before I got the job dancing in Jubilee, I had a lot of time on my hands. Patrick had unintentionally introduced me to adult bookstores and glory holes in Vegas. We were not in an open relationship, but we enjoyed playing with others together. He brought me to my first bookstore and I was hooked. I don't know what it was, but there was something so dirty and depraved but sexy about going into a smelly bookstore. Even now when I smell the stench of the cheap lemon cleaner most of them use, it's familiar and comforting. I would go in, stick my dick through a hole, and someone on the other side would suck me off. I loved it. Something about the anonymity of it all turned me on so much. I had no interest in meeting guys online or in bars, but bookstores and glory holes suited me well. It was quick, easy and there were generally little to no questions asked. My favorite time to go was around four or five in the afternoon when all the married men would be stopping in to get blowjobs after work. These men would come in dressed in their casual business attire with raging hard-ons ready to be sucked off. I'm not sure if any of them were gay or bisexual but they were more than willing to let a little blond boy suck their dicks, and I would eagerly get on my knees and do so. To this day, nothing turns me on more than a glory hole bookstore encounter. If I'm ever with a client or shooting porn, and need to get myself aroused or climax, all I do is think back to the days of trolling the arcades, sucking off countless guys. I had to stop going when all my favorite adult bookstores started playing my porn in the booths, and some of the guys I was with would look at the porn and me and say, "Hey... isn't that you?" I usually said no, but sometimes I admitted it. I don't think they understood why the guy on the TV fucking the hot porn star would be in a sleazy, dirty, smelly bookstore in the middle of the day. It wasn't something I wanted to discuss, so I would brush it off casually and shut them up by sucking their dicks, or grabbing their heads and shoving my cock down their throats.

A year after I started filming porn, I was walking down Eighth Avenue in New York City, and I went into one of the bookstores on my way back to my hotel. I had two clients earlier that day and then went to a bar called the Eagle which is where I usually end up when I visit New York City. That day, I still hadn't had my fill of sex, so I figured I would stop in, get off, and be on my way.

The clerk at the front of the store was breaking a ten-dollar bill when a drunk-looking guy approached me. He said (very loudly), "Hey... I know who you are. You're Christopher Daniels! I saw on Twitter that you'd be in New York City, so I sent you an email about meeting up. Why didn't you respond to me?"

Pissed off that he was about to ruin my anonymous bookstore encounter, I gave him a dirty look and said, "Seriously, buddy?" I realize we were in a bookstore on Eighth Avenue at 3 a.m. and looking to get our dicks sucked, but I was under the assumption that most people knew that little talking was done in an establishment like this and hoped he would leave me alone so I could get off and leave. I went into the arcade area and gave a friendly nod to a few guys before locking myself in a booth, hoping the drunk guy wouldn't find me. Fortunately, he didn't, but he did come stumbling into the arcade area knocking on the video booth doors asking "Where's that blond pornstar? I wanna talk to him!" It was then I realized that unless I was incognito, usually wearing sunglasses or at least a hat, I probably couldn't go into a bookstore for an anonymous blowjob without some drunk guy pointing out who I was.

Although I enjoyed going to these places alone, Patrick and I sometimes went to the bathhouses and bookstores together. A couple months after we started going I made it clear that I wanted to go on my own sometimes. He hated this, but I think he felt he had no control over it and was afraid to lose me, so he let me do what I wanted. The sex between us had gotten boring and it didn't excite me anymore. I needed something new. Being sexually active was still fairly new to me, and I loved the release in these anonymous encounters without him.

During my four years with Patrick, I started watching porn produced by one of the most controversial companies in the industry, Treasure Island Media (TIM). One day, I came home to find a few DVDs Patrick had ordered. One of them was called *Animals* and the other one was called *What I Can't See*. Until this, my porn taste was pretty vanilla and not too extreme, but after watching *Animals*—which has absolutely nothing to do with bestiality, but about men who are so horny they have sex like animals in heat—I was hooked on Treasure Island Media porn.

After frequenting bookstores and bathhouses, I started watching Treasure Island Media's *Drunk On Cum* series of movies where one lucky guy would be on the floor in the middle of a group of guys—anywhere from two to twenty or more—and basically suck them all off until they came in his mouth or on his face. This whole fantasy clicked within me, and I became obsessed with oral sex. It was all very depraved, and some might view it as sick or twisted, but I didn't care. It groomed me to be a complete cocksucking whore, and it felt great.

One night, I was determined to go to a bookstore and collect as many loads as I could either on my face or mouth. I don't know what it is, but there is something thrilling about guys cumming in my mouth and on my face and——in a way——humiliating and degrading me. I don't think of it as doing something I don't want to do or I wouldn't have repeatedly done it. I thought it was hot and I would fully let whoever wanted to cum on my face or in my mouth do so, zip up, and leave.

31

One evening I was on a mission to suck as much dick as possible at my favorite bookstore in Las Vegas. The place was pretty busy and I hid inside one of the booths and waited for guys to pace up and down the halls. The first guy I saw was a shorter Mexican guy with a cowboy hat and white boots. He looked like he just hopped over the border and landed in Vegas. He had a thin mustache and looked like he didn't speak a word of English, which was perfect in my mind. It was usually better if we didn't speak to each other.

I motioned for him to come into the booth. Right away, he grabbed his hard dick and motioned for me to suck it. I got down on my knees and began sucking his beautiful uncut seven-inch cock. He obviously loved it and came within a few minutes. He zipped up his pants, smiled, said something in Spanish, and left. The taste of his cum lingered in the back of my throat and it felt great. It tasted like the drip you get in the back of your throat after snorting a line of cocaine—kind of bitter, but I liked it. The aftertaste made my dick even harder, and I was onto the next guy. I sucked off six guys that night and probably spent a total of two hours in there. I felt like one of the depraved sex addicts I read about in my ex-gay ministry reading material, but I didn't care. After the sixth guy blew his load in my mouth, I couldn't hold back any longer and I shot a huge load all over the floor of the booth before collapsing on the padded bench. The last guy I was with wanted me to go to his hotel with him and spend the night, but I was not interested. I was there to suck dick, not find a boyfriend. I had a boyfriend at home and that was enough.

During the years of cruising bookstores, my relationship with Patrick became very strained. We had a codependent cycle and neither one could break it because it was comfortable for both of us. I desperately wanted to be taken care of, and Patrick loved being the caretaker. We had a nice life together with two cars, two dogs, and a brand-new house. Life was pretty much perfect, except the fact that we never had sex anymore and had become completely distant emotionally and physically. I was twenty-three when I had met Patrick, and I was now in my late twenties. I had changed as a person and didn't want to be tied down in a relationship I wasn't fully invested in. I think Patrick felt this, too, but he didn't want to admit it. He was used to being the caretaker and liked that role. Without it he seemed lost, and I felt like I was continuing with the relationship simply because we had so much invested, and I didn't know how to break away. I truly did love him but I knew love wasn't enough to stay together if things were clearly not working.

One night we were out partying with friends of mine from Jubilee. It took a lot of convincing Patrick to go out with us because he had grown so content with just staying home, working around the house or watching television and relaxing. If we did go out, it was usually to a low-key place where we would have a few beers, play pool, and talk with friends. I was still into going out to clubs, drinking until dawn, going for breakfast, and then passing out around eight or nine in the morning. It was Las Vegas after all. This is how most of us spent our time when we went out. Patrick would put up with it and act like he was having fun, but I knew he wasn't. We had been out to the popular gay club on the strip called Krave and then headed to a hole-in-the-wall bar called the Buffalo. I was there with my friends Monica, Brent, and Jacob. Jacob had a fresh stash of cocaine and was sharing it freely with everyone. Hard drugs weren't something I did often, but once in a while when out dancing at clubs, I would indulge if they were offered. Patrick was against all drugs except weed. He didn't even like knowing I had done them in my past, so the few times I took part, I had to hide it from him.

Jacob and I were going back and forth to the bathroom doing lines on the back of the toilet with a dollar bill, and also continuing to drink and chain-smoke all night. The more coke I did, the more I needed to maintain my high. I asked Jacob for the bag, and I went to the bathroom to do another line. I spread it on top of the toilet tank and cut it into a few neat lines with a credit card. I was sick of making trips to the bathroom and worried Patrick would start asking questions, so I wanted to snort enough to maintain a good high for the rest of the night. As I bent over to snort the huge line, I saw my reflection in the giant mirror in front of me. I snorted the first line and then waited a few seconds before I went for the second. As I snorted it, I suddenly saw Patrick's reflection in the mirror walking into the bathroom. I had stupidly forgotten to lock the door. He saw me, acted surprised, and said, "Oh, sorry," before dashing out. I stood up over the toilet and knew he had seen me. I started freaking out thinking, *Oh my God. He's going to kill me.* I waited a few seconds, sat on the toilet and collapsed my face into my hands and whispered, "SHIT." I didn't know what to do. Patrick had clearly seen me snorting a line, but for some reason, he hadn't acted like he knew what I was doing or who I was. Instead, he just had just given me a funny look and acted embarrassed for walking into the bathroom. *Maybe he didn't recognize me?* I took a moment to calm down, snorted the last line, washed my hands, grabbed my drink, and walked out to face whatever was waiting for me outside the bathroom.

Patrick smiled at me and said, "Hey, I didn't realize it was you in there." He had come and left so quickly he must not have seen my face. He looked at me strangely and asked, "Are you okay?"

"Yeah, yeah, yeah... totally," I sniffed nervously, still unsure if I was in the clear. He looked confused, almost as if he knew something was up, but he had no clue what was going on.

"Are you having fun?" I asked.

"Yeah, it's OK. I think I'm ready to go soon."

"OK, sure," I responded.

He looked closer at me, and after a few seconds he asked, "Christopher, what's under your nose?"

Shit. I was totally busted. I quickly wiped my nose and said, "Nothing, why?"

"That's it!" he screamed. "Get your shit. We're going home now!" As he stormed out the front door, I peeked in the bathroom mirror at my face and saw white powder in both nostrils and above my lips. I looked like a complete junkie and a total sweaty mess. I turned a ghostly shade of white, my knees became weak, and I felt sick to my stomach.

"Fuck," I said, then cleaned myself up and ran after Patrick.

On the drive home, he broke up with me and told me I had to get out of the house. I packed a few bags silently, still completely fucked up and coked out. I had no idea where to go, so I went back to the Buffalo to see if my friends were still there. I met up with Brent and Jacob and told them everything that happened. Jacob took us back to his house, where we did line after line of coke, and I spent the entire time sobbing. They continued to console me as we snorted lines off a dinner plate until the wee hours of the morning.

Although Patrick had threatened before to break up with me, this time I knew it was over. I needed to move on and start a new life again, ending this dysfunctional codependent relationship cycle.

Chapter Four

Money, Travel and Sex

Clients and friends often ask me why I started escorting. One word: money. Any escort that tells you they do it for another reason is probably lying. Some claim they do it because they love sex so much and need it all the time. There's probably some truth to that, but escorts are not banging guys that look like Richard Gere in the movie *Pretty Woman*, so it's going to take a lot more than an overwhelming need for sex or being a sex addict to be working as an escort in this industry.

The reason I began was because I needed money and I needed it quick. When Patrick and I broke up, I was left in a position where I needed my own place to live. We had bought a house together a few years earlier, but the house was in his name.

It was 2009, and Las Vegas was in the middle of the housing crisis. Decent-sized homes in good condition were going for anywhere from $100,000 to $125, 000. I knew with my credit and job history that I could buy a condo or a small house. The monthly mortgage payments would be a lot cheaper than renting a place, but I needed to come up with a few thousand dollars for a down payment. I was still dancing in Jubilee at Bally's Hotel, making a decent salary. My credit rating was good, but I did not have money lying around for a down payment or closing costs to purchase a home. Not only that, but I knew buying a home was going to require additional money to get started with some simple renovations and to purchase appliances. I couldn't borrow the money from anyone I knew, so the answer seemed simple... become a male escort, a "Rentboy."

I was intrigued by the thought of what it would be like to have sex with people for money. I loved having sex so much in my personal life that some would consider me a borderline sex addict. I thought why not transform my dysfunction into cash? A part of me dreamed of a life of dinners with rich clients in nice restaurants, or flying around the world for fun getaways with billionaires. The life of an escort was glamorous, or at least the movie *Pretty Woman* made it seem that way.

I had been offered money for sex a few times on online hook-up sites and actually done it once when Patrick and I moved to Las Vegas in 2006 and we needed cash. I had already spent all my savings moving and purchasing our apartment (next to the Hard Rock Casino) and its furniture. One night, a married man in his fifties contacted me through a popular hook-up site called Manhunt and we began chatting. I was bored and drunk on apple pucker martinis, so I was humoring him, flirting to pass the time until Patrick got home from work. Our messages went from playful to sexual, and he finally asked if I would come over and have sex with him for three hundred dollars. *Three hundred bucks just to have sex with him? How can I say no?* I was drunk, thinking only about the money and not my boyfriend or my safety, and I stumbled over to his hotel, just across the street. He met me outside and walked me to his room. He was playing porn and the lights were low. The guy wasn't especially attractive, but he wasn't ugly either. He was an overweight middle-aged man, but he took care of himself, smelled good, and was polite. Years later, when I began escorting full-time, I realized how little things like good hygiene and manners, so simple in my mind, were often rare. We walked into the room, and I didn't feel nervous or scared. I knew what I had come there to do, so I undressed and got hard immediately. The thrill and excitement of this whole situation was enough to make my dick stand straight up and smack against my stomach. I felt like I was doing something bad and I loved it. It wasn't as if I was really into the guy, but I definitely got off on the fact that this man got off on me. A trait of a typical narcissist. He sucked my dick for about five minutes, I sucked his dick for a few more, and then I jerked off until we came. I got dressed, he gave me my three hundred dollars, and I was on my way home. It was the easiest money I had ever made! I put it toward bills and phone cards to call my family over the next few days.

The guilt eventually set in, however. A few months later, when I was really drunk, I broke down and told Patrick everything. He was furious and threatened to dump me that night, but we somehow worked through it and stayed together. Our dysfunctional codependent relationship lasted three more years.

A few days after Patrick and I split for good, he told me he wanted to try to make our relationship work and he didn't want to give up. I contemplated it for a while because we had built a life for ourselves, owned a nice new home, and had two dogs together. I did love him, but in my heart I knew it was time to move on, grow up, and be on my own. I needed to figure out how to be an adult and quit asking Patrick to take care of me. I knew I couldn't begin to do this unless I was on my own, supporting myself financially and emotionally away from him.

Now I had to embark on this journey as a single man in my late twenties without going into too much debt while still living the standard of living I was used to. The answer seemed simple: Become an escort. In the next few weeks, I put an ad on a popular male escort site called Rentboy and started taking calls. Within a month I had money for a down payment, closing costs, and some home renovations.

Was I sacrificing my morals? Am I a bad person for doing what I was doing? Was I inevitably going to get an STD and die strung out on something, like men in every single bad movie made about male hustlers? Was I going to be working a corner in some seedy neighborhood like Hunter, that kid with HIV on the television show *Queer As Folk*? I didn't know, and I honestly didn't care. I wanted money and I had found an easy way to get it.

So obviously I chose the path of escorting—and later porn—because of money. I wanted money and I wanted a lot of it. But in doing what I am doing I have gone further than just making money. I have been able to use sex as a way to connect with others and make them feel special. When I started out, I never expected to have any influence or impact on other people's lives, and I feel blessed to have done so. Of course, the money is the reason I started and the reason I continue, but it means a lot to me when I make a difference in someone's life and give them a memorable experience they hopefully never forget.

A few months ago, I met a man who had had a partner for over twenty years. He told me they had been faithful to each other and monogamous the entire time they were together. His partner had died seventeen years earlier, and since then he had not been involved sexually with anyone. He called me because he was finally in a place where he needed a physical connection, and he was ready to start letting himself be intimate with others. He saw both my ad and porn online and decided to ask me to help him through this process of sexual intimacy. As soon as he told me this story, I felt flattered and then an immense amount of pressure. *WOW! Me? Really? Okay... sure.* It's almost spiritual and too much to handle. I gave him a sensual and passionate experience and he was near tears because of the intensity of it all. We talked in bed for another hour and a half. I asked him questions about his life, his partner, his home in Santa Fe, and the type of work he does. I was also intrigued as to how someone goes without sex for over seventeen years. He also asked a lot of questions about me. He was genuinely interested in who I was, why I escort, where I came from, my family, relationships, and my plans for the future. I began to feel like I was in therapy as I talked about my childhood, ex-boyfriends, and family members. Instead of me paying him eighty dollars an hour to listen, like I did with my therapist, he was paying me three hundred an hour to play the role of the therapist and give me advice and his perspective on things. Times like this are invaluable and have left a mark on me.

While I do believe that the money is what makes escorts start in this industry, having meaningful connections with others gives us longevity and keeps us from going insane. I have met and worked with dozens of other men in this business and, for the most part, I have met some great guys. They are hardworking, genuine, caring people with intense sex drives. Of course there are also some strung-out tweakers, ready and willing to do anything for cash. In my opinion, if you come into this industry with a level head, recognize it for what it is, and have a back-up plan for when you can't escort anymore, you will be fine. If you let all the compliments, attention, cash, and recognition go to your head, get ready for a downward spiral that will not end well.

Chapter Five

Testing My Limits

I left the Blue Moon Resort after a two-hour appointment. I had just spent the afternoon with a regular client I saw named Gary, from San Francisco, a great guy I had seen almost every other month for the past year. The times with him were always low-maintenance and easy-going but sometimes being with anyone for more than an hour can be exhausting. I genuinely enjoyed Gary and he had become a big part of my life as an escort and porn star the year before when I had first met him. He was definitely my number one fan and treated me like gold. I first met him when he came to Las Vegas the previous year three days after the funeral of his partner of eighteen years passed away. Our first meeting was a little odd, seeing as we were meeting a few days after his partner's funeral and I could tell he was obviously going through a lot. I sensed that he was doing whatever he could to not break down under the pressure of the death of a loved one, and what perfect way to do that than to schedule a few hours with a male escort. Sex really is a great stress reliever. Our meetings were low-maintenance, and I didn't feel like it was anything out of the ordinary or life-changing, but for some reason, he had taken a liking to me. As time went on, he became special to me and I was special to him. During one of our meetings after seeing each other for almost a year, he became very emotional and told me how much I meant to him. He knew we had a client/escort relationship, and it wasn't as if he had fallen in love with me, but for some reason, our times together had helped him through one of the darkest periods of his life after his partner died. I had no idea what I had ever done or said to make him feel that way, because I felt like all we ever did was make small talk and then engage in very innocent sexual activity. For some reason, though, that was enough for him and it helped him gain confidence in himself as a newly single man in his sixties.

After saying good-bye to Gary I walked into the parking lot and I got into my car. I had thirty minutes to get to the Imperial Palace

Theater to go over the choreography for the show that night; I was cast in the show *Divas,* where I worked as a fill-in dancer when the regular full-time dancers were sick or took a vacation day. I was usually scheduled in the show once or twice a week, so this worked great with escorting, film shoots, and traveling, but it was awful for my brain. If I don't do a show full-time or consistently drill choreography from a show into my memory, I forget everything. This had caused some problems for me in the show, but I was still hanging in there based on my looks, height, body, and the fact that they desperately needed a male dancer that would work for the ridiculously low salary they were offering. I was definitely not doing the show for the money; it was a way for me to continue dancing in a show and not just work as a Rentboy or porn star. I still equated a lot of my self-worth with what I did for a living, and at that point in my life I was not ready to stop being a dancer. It was all I knew and it was such a big part of my identity, I couldn't give it up yet.

As I got into my car, the phone rang from a 646 area code. I didn't recognize the number and I had no idea who it was. He told me his name was Tim and he wanted to set up an appointment. He was coming to Las Vegas in a few weeks and wanted to set something up for the afternoon of May 2, at the Aria Casino and Resort.

On the day of our meeting, I showed up to the Aria at four in the afternoon, as scheduled. I knocked on the door and a man talking on the phone answers. Right away, my focus went directly to the nose area. I noticed one problem: He didn't have a nose! The area was covered by a patch of what looked like snakeskin. Immediately I thought, *What the fuck is going on? Run, Christopher, run! Don't look back, just run! Why is this man missing his nose? How does this even happen? Where did it go? What's under the patch? Oh, my God, I think I'm going to be physically ill if that patch falls off.*

Tim sounded like he was dealing with some kind of emergency and something bad had happened. He motioned for me to sit down while he is dealing with an obviously serious phone call, so I hesitantly sat down, but refused to make myself comfortable. I thought to myself, *"This is it, Christopher. For the first time, I am going to scream and BOLT out of a meeting with a client. I will throw up, cry, and then call my friend Bobby as I sob to him about how I met a man with a missing nose.* At the same time, something inside me said, *Sit your ass down. You have no clue what may happen. You can leave if you want, but at least give it a chance.*

He finished the call and immediately launched into the story of how his mother had fallen and hurt herself that morning. He was consoling her, but she was upset and bedridden in the hospital. He then complained about a slight tear on one of the living room chairs and his overall disappointment with the hotel. He was acting like he was being forced to stay in a Motel 6, even though it was the newest and one of the nicest hotel on the Las Vegas strip. The tear was obviously irritating him because he mentioned that he planned to discuss it with the management. All the while I was thinking, *WHAT THE FUCK IS UP WITH YOUR NOSE? Quit acting like this is normal. It's not!*

He sat down, smiled, looked at me affectionately, paused, and then said, "So I guess you're wondering about my nose."

I nodded and said as calmly as possible, "Yes, I am."

He explained that he had developed skin cancer on his nose so severe that the entire nose had to be removed.

PLEASE do not let this patch fall off. I will literally be sick everywhere if I see a hole in his face, I kept thinking.

"My friend decided to make me a patch made out of snakeskin after I had my nose removed. Would you like to touch it?"

He grabbed my hand and guided it to his nose, but I pulled my hand away and said, "Please don't. I really hate snakes." I do hate snakes more than anything, but the idea of touching a scaly snakeskin patch that was covering a hole on his face was too much for one day.

He said okay and smiled. I was trying my best to not reveal the panic brewing within my stomach. We were five minutes into the meeting, and I knew this would be my greatest acting challenge yet. I have an incredibly weak stomach and even seeing a kid wiggle a loose tooth will make me nauseous, so I had a very hard time making sense of this situation or figuring out what I should do. I have been with a few clients who had physical impairments, and I have been with countless men who were severely overweight and had various skin conditions. I was used to unexpected surprises with my clients where I had to quickly adapt. One time I had to spend three hours with a man weighing over three hundred pounds who was also missing half his chest due to Poland's Syndrome, with the worst case of psoriasis on his legs I have ever seen. Parts of his legs had literally turned brown and purple due to his skin condition, but I somehow made it through the three hours of him touching me and rubbing the scaly skin against mine. I'm not sure how I made it through some of these meetings, but I felt like I had no choice and tried not to focus on whatever it was that was bothering me. My job is to affirm these men, make them comfortable, and accept them for who they are, physically and emotionally. I always do my best, but I'm not going to lie and say sometimes it wasn't difficult.

This missing nose thing was not sitting well with me, but I didn't want to appear uneasy or freaked out. Inside, I was falling apart. Obviously, this man called me for a reason, and I knew it was time to start what I came here to do.

I had taken a Viagra before I came over just in case, and the side effect of congestion in my sinuses was starting to kick in. Viagra affects everyone differently, but I knew it was working for me when I started to feel the congestion and sinus pressure. Even though my head was beginning to feel stuffy, I didn't have a rock-hard erection. Viagra usually always works on me unless I am emotionally or physically upset about something. I couldn't get all the possible pictures of what was underneath the snakeskin patch out of my head.

He leaned in to kiss me, and so it began. I tried to focus on anything. I thought of the hottest porn I have ever seen, some of the hottest men I have slept with, and that time I blew six guys and they all shot their loads in my mouth and on my face at a local bookstore. I was trying to think of the hottest scenarios and sexual experiences I've ever had but all I kept thinking was, *I pray to God that patch doesn't fall off, forcing me to look at the hole in his face.* We decided to move into the bedroom, and I was trying not to think of what he might want to do. Maybe he would be one of those clients I could just suck off, kiss, and finish off with a hand-job within ten minutes, but something in my gut told me this guy wanted more. He undressed and I undressed, and we got on the bed and began to kiss. Other than missing a nose, he was a decent-looking man in his fifties, and I couldn't help but wonder what he once looked like. Missing something that is usually there (like a nose) really changes the entire structure of one's face. He flipped me over and began eating my ass, and all I could think was, *This man is rubbing his scaly snakeskin patch in between my ass cheeks as he licks my hole with his tongue, deeper and deeper inside me. How is this even happening, and how is this my fucking life?* I couldn't make sense of anything going on, and I knew this was a time when I was seriously contemplating leaving escorting. I was freaking out and didn't want to be there. He continued to eat me out and shove his face in deeper and deeper like he was trying to suck something out of my asshole with his mouth.

He flipped me over and began sucking my dick. The Viagra kicked in and I had a semi hard-on, enough to pass off as an erection. Every few minutes or so, I would look down at him just to be sure the patch was still on his face and there was no gaping hole visible. This man loved sucking cock and he eagerly went to town on my dick for at least ten minutes. He was ready to start fucking so he reached for the condoms and lube and offered me some. Did he sense my uneasiness? Could he tell that I was on the verge of screaming or crying, and I desperately did not want to be there? Did he go through this with all his escorts, or was I the only one who felt this squeamish? I felt like my head was literally going to combust, with the combination of all the thoughts going through my mind and the Viagra congestion.

I climbed on top of him and he put his dick in my ass. It slid in easily and I hoped for no more than two minutes of thrusts before he shot his load on my back. Then I would be on my way. Unfortunately, this guy was definitely getting his money's worth, and he fucked me for at least five minutes before asking to fuck me from behind. I readily agreed so I wouldn't have to look at the snakeskin. He fucked me for a little bit more before he stopped and said, "Okay, that's enough. Now we're going to have a talk."

What the fuck was going on? Talk about what? I just looked at him as he ripped the condom off and threw it in the garbage bin.

He sat down next to me and I stared at him as he laughed and said, "This is probably the weirdest escorting situation you have ever been in, right?"

"To be honest, it probably is."

"I've been following your work for a while and I planned this trip to meet you."

"OK. You've been following my work and planned a trip just to meet me?" I repeated, to make sure I had understood him correctly.

"Well, I came to the West Coast for business, but one of the reasons I came to Vegas was to meet you."

"I see..." How do you even begin to react to something like that?

"I organize meetings for a gay couple who loves escorts. My job is to find them and refer them to my clients. If they approve, then we will fly you to New York City, or wherever they are staying, to meet for a three-hour period and you will be paid three thousand dollars."

"For only three hours?"

"Yes," he said. "We will fly you out the day before, and the following afternoon, you will spend an afternoon with them and a few other escorts. It'll be fun. I promise my clients are very low-maintenance. The next day we will fly you back home. Does this sound like something you would be interested in?"

"Sure," I said. Was he serious? Three hours, three thousand dollars, and a trip to New York?

A couple times a month, I will get a phone call from somebody who offers me something that sounds too good to be true. And it usually is. I've been offered flights around the world, cruises, trips to see clients who will pay ten thousand dollars (or more) for a weekend together, people asking me for my address so they can send clothes, cologne, and underwear. I've been contacted by Saudi Arabian royalty (or so they claimed) and people who work for some of the most famous actors in Hollywood. Unfortunately, when it comes time for these guys to follow through, none of them do. In this business, the majority of the people were lying and I just stopped counting on anything anyone promises.

"You think I'm full of shit, don't you?" he asked.

"To be honest," I replied, "I think everyone is full of shit until the money is in my hands or at least a plane ticket has been purchased in my name."

"OK, I'll submit your pictures and let you know. You will probably need to take Viagra when you meet the guys. You seemed a little soft during our meeting and they like the guys to have hard-ons." I wanted to tell him I couldn't get fully erect because I was too focused on the hole in his face, but I just smiled and nodded. "Also, be sure not to act effeminate. Butch it up a bit. The client doesn't like feminine guys." I wanted to smack the patch right off his face for saying that, but again I just smiled and agreed. I knew I wasn't the most masculine guy but I didn't think I was a limp-wristed queen.

We showered together and continued talking as I got dressed. Every time I asked him questions about who he worked for, he smiled and was very vague in his responses. There were a lot of unanswered questions about this arrangement, but to be honest, I didn't care. I refused to get my hopes anymore, even though the idea of three thousand dollars for a three-hour appointment sounded amazing. He said he would be in touch, and I collected my money and left.

The next day, he asked by text if I would be interested in going to Paris that weekend. I said sure but, again, refused to believe it was going to happen until I had a plane ticket with my name on it. He asked for my full name and address, and after just three hours, he sent me a tentative itinerary for a flight to Paris and told me I would receive three thousand dollars the next day along with three hundred euros for cab and food money while I was there. This man sounded more and more serious, but it wasn't until FedEx showed up the next morning with an envelope stuffed with cash that I knew he was not full of shit.

Three days later, I boarded a plane and went to Paris to meet these mystery clients Tim had told me about. He followed through on everything he had mentioned. Even though I spent more time traveling than in Paris, the trip went well. Plus, I was pleased to learn there were still a few people left in the world who kept their word and followed through with their promises.

Chapter Six

The Non-Typical Virgin

I received an e-mail from a guy named Craig. He was coming to Las Vegas the first week of 2011 and would be staying at the Luxor Hotel. He was interested in setting up an appointment with me for three hours. When he asked how much it would cost, I told him I would charge him only two hundred dollars per hour, a discount for the multiple hours. We exchanged some e-mails back and forth, and as we continued to correspond, he told me that he suffered from multiple sclerosis. He said he had no mobility of his body below his neck and would be coming to Las Vegas with a caregiver to help him out. He wanted to know if I would be comfortable with this. At first, I didn't know how to respond. In the back of my mind, I knew one day I would get an offer from someone with major physical restrictions and I would have to decide if I was comfortable with it or not. At that time, I was dating another escort, Jason Michaels. We had been seeing each other almost daily for a few months, and our time together was causing us both to neglect clients and lose out on money we were used to making. It was putting a strain on our relationship. Making six hundred dollars, especially after the holidays and a week after I had just bought a new car, would help things out for me financially. I looked at meeting someone with severe physical restrictions as a challenge and told myself it would be, if nothing else, a new experience. It was as if I was embarking on something many escorts eventually have to do at one time or another, and my time had come.

I told Craig his physical condition would not be a problem and I was excited to meet him. To be honest, I had no clue if his physical condition would be a problem, but I guess we would figure it out when I got there. The last thing I wanted to do was make him feel self-conscious especially since he told me our visit would be the highlight of his trip. To think that I could bring joy to someone who couldn't even get out of bed, eat, or urinate on his own, made me feel incredibly humble and small.

The day of the meeting, my roommate Brigitte from France informed me she was unhappy with the living situation and didn't want to stay in my house anymore. She said she didn't like Jason or his dogs and she was going to find her own apartment. I had no clue what to say to her when she told me this. She had always seemed uptight about Jason staying in the house and had made it clear she didn't like his dogs. Numerous times, I had gone out of my way to accommodate her and her financial situation, but I guess it still wasn't working for her. She said she would be out of the house within a few weeks, and that was that. She told me this as I was tying my shoes and on my way out the door. I was speechless and completely caught off guard but didn't have the time or energy to discuss it with her, so I picked up my bag and left. I had always thought we were friends, and I was left feeling hurt and angry.Hearing bad news or having conflict before a meeting with a client is awful, and I needed to focus on my client and his three-hour session.

I drove to the Luxor Hotel and parked my brand-new 2010 Dodge Challenger. I felt like such a rock star in my car, but I found it odd on that particular day that I was going to make my first car payment using money I made by spending time with a man who was practically paralyzed. *If people only knew...* I climbed out of the car and packed my bag full of everything I would need: lube, condoms, body lotion, water bottle, poppers, and a change of clothes for the gym later—typical escorting supplies.

I wandered around the Luxor until I found his room, which was hidden away in a separate area of the hotel with large handicapped-equipped suites.

I knocked on the door, and a good-looking younger guy smoking a cigarette answered. I had no clue who he was, but he smiled and shook my hand. He introduced himself as Craig's nurse, and then led me to meet Craig. I was hoping he was going to stay behind and that maybe Craig only wanted to see us play together. This was something that didn't happen too often, but every once in a while a client will hire me and another escort—or sometimes two, three, four, or even five—and just watch us play together as he got off. Having sex with other escorts and hot porn stars kind of felt like you hit the jackpot and would make me think You're going to pay me to do what?" I walked into the room and finally met Craig, and I'm not sure anything could have prepared me for the severity of his condition. I had never met anyone with multiple sclerosis, except the wife of a pastor at the church I went to growing up. She was always in good spirits and could walk and seemed in relatively good health. I knew there were different types of multiple sclerosis, but I didn't realize there was one that left you bedridden, paralyzed, and attached to tubes and machines. Craig's nurse put out his cigarette, gathered his laptop, smiled, and excused himself. I wanted to say to him, *Please don't leave. I have no clue how to handle any of this stuff, let alone try to be sexy, calm, and have sex with a man who can't move.*

The door closed behind him and we were alone. I smiled at Craig and he offered me a seat.

"How's it going?" I asked, trying to sound relaxed, in control, and completely okay with the situation, even though I was completely freaked out by the machines everywhere.

"Really good. Thanks for coming," he said.

"Of course. I am glad I was able to make it."

"So, I sort of told you a little bit about my condition."

"Right, you have multiple sclerosis?"

"Yes."

"When did this happen? Were you born with it?"

"I have a disease called primary progressive multiple sclerosis. I was diagnosed with it at the age of twenty and went from a 'normal' twenty-year-old to a quadriplegic in a little under seven years. My condition is related to multiple sclerosis, which a lot of people are familiar with, but mine is a bit different. While both the standard MS and the primary progressive versions share the same disease process of one's own immune system, attacking the thin layer of fat insulating nerves allowing them to properly transmit their signals called the myelin sheath." It sounded like he was reciting a textbook, and I'm sure he was. He must have gone through explaining his condition to a lot of people over the years, but most likely I was the first escort he was explaining it to.

"I hope I'm not boring you," he said.

"Not at all. I don't really understand a lot of what you are saying, but it's all very interesting."

He laughed, smiled, and continued explaining. "Primary progressive attacks are much quicker, whereas standard relapsing, or remitting, as it is properly called, can take literally decades to cause the kind of damage I experienced in a few short years. But I still have many blessings in my life, such as the disease essentially stopping its progression for close to ten years now after turning me into a quadriplegic, which means my brain is unaffected and I still have many other pretty much unimpeded functions... and I guess sex is one of them, which is why I called you."

"So your condition hasn't affected your ability to have an orgasm or feel things?"

"Exactly... and I didn't actually come out of the closet until I was twenty-three. By then, I had lost all mobility of my lower body and couldn't move. You remind me of this guy I knew in high school, which is why I contacted you. He was so gorgeous and I used to fantasize about him and jerk off to him all the time. I've never actually been with a guy before, so this will be my first experience."

"You've never been with a guy ever?"

"Nope, never," he laughed.

"So you mean you've never kissed a guy, blew a friend, or jerked off with another guy as a teenager?"

"Nope, sorry," he laughed.

I thought I was a late bloomer sexually, especially compared to most gay men I knew. By the time I was sixteen, I had at least kissed a guy, made out with another, sucked a guy off, and given at least half a dozen hand-jobs at random sleepovers or drunken parties in high school. It was hard for me to comprehend how a guy could know he was gay his whole life but never act on it once.

"Funny story, though: I used to be a phone sex operator."

"After you couldn't move anymore?"

"Yup," he laughed.

Wow, this meeting was definitely not what I was expecting.

"So what are you wanting to do today? What can you do?" I asked. I still had no idea how I was going to pull this off and try to give him at least some mild sexual satisfaction.

"Well, I wanted to kiss you, have you touch me and suck my dick, and I want to fuck you. I don't think I'll be able to get fucked..." When he said that, I thought, *I'm not even sure how we're going to do the majority of what you just mentioned, let alone me fucking you.* I guess it was going to be trial and error until he shot a load or at least until the clock said 4 p.m.

"Would it be okay if we started with a light massage?" he asked.

"Sure, that works," I replied.

"So what do you do back in Illinois?" I asked as I began to undress and get the body lotion out of my bag.

"I'm actually studying to be a lawyer"

"Wow, that's impressive!" I couldn't believe someone that had so many things going against him had the will and drive to become a lawyer. If I have a day where my face breaks out or my body dimorphism creeps up on me, and I feel hideous, I can barely get out of bed or leave my house without a hat on.

Craig asked to be covered by the sheets on at least his upper body, and so he lied there as I spread some lotion on his legs and messaged them underneath the blankets. He closed his eyes and I could tell he already loved every minute of it. I couldn't understand as a gay man, how you could go your entire life without sharing an intimate experience with another man, yet still know you were gay. As an escort, there were so many days where I felt oversexed and physically exhausted, and sometimes the thought of someone touching me or getting fucked, yet again felt like a bad hangover and literally made me want to throw up. Despite everything Craig had going against him, I could tell he didn't want my pity, but my heart sank as I touched his lifeless legs. I couldn't understand how he seemed pretty happy and content in his life despite not being able to do much of anything on his own.

My hands went higher and higher on his legs and I could see as I passed his knees that the sheets and blankets were making a tent around his dick. *Wow,* I thought, *I guess his equipment really does work!* I continued to massage closer and closer to his balls until I finally took his dick in my hand and began to stroke it. *So this is what a dick that hasn't gotten off in years feels like.*

Although this session was already a little emotionally draining, I was intrigued by it all. I was in a room at the Luxor Hotel having sex with a virgin who had multiple sclerosis and couldn't move his body. I wasn't sure what made him choose the Luxor, as it is one of the least desirable places to stay on the strip. As I continued to massage him I asked why, and he told me that between his trip to Vegas with his caregiver and hiring me, the Luxor was all he could afford. That made my heart melt even more, and I felt guilty knowing I was going to take his money at the end of our session.

I applied a bit more lotion to my hands and kept stroking his dick slowly. I'm not sure how close he was to cumming, but I wanted to at least try getting him through oral and anal sex so he could get his money's worth and enjoy himself. I lifted up the sheets, took his dick in my hands, bent down to wrap my lips around it and began to suck. Instantly, he began to moan. Now I was curious. I had forgotten how a blowjob feels for the first time. I get one or give one almost every day, so it was interesting to see how someone his age reacts to getting blown for the first time ever. I went at it for a few minutes and tried my best to make it as sensual and enjoyable as possible.

He asked if he could kiss me, and I said sure. Honestly though, I was debating whether this was something I was okay doing. Typically, I always kiss clients for a little bit, unless they stink like cigarette smoke, are missing teeth, or have terrible halitosis. Many people think escorts never kiss because it's too personal, but they'll do almost anything else. My clients generally hire me for a boyfriend experience and want more than rough, hard, nasty, or messy sex. They generally want something sensual, romantic, and passionate, so I always try at least a little bit of kissing. With Craig, there were cords connected to machines that were attached to his body, and he couldn't really move his head, so I went in and began kissing his mouth and he lay there looking up at me as he experienced his first kiss with a man. The whole experience so far was anything but typical. Again I wanted to give him an experience to remember, so I continued kissing him for a few minutes and he seemed to really enjoy it.

He was eager to get to the fucking, but I could tell he wanted to spend an equal amount of time kissing, being touched, and just feeling another man next to him. I asked him if he wanted to eat my ass, and he said sure. I looked around the bed to see what I could use for balance. Even though he was going to be giving me the rim job, this was going to take some thought on my part.

I managed to balance myself over his head with one foot on the nightstand and another foot on the bed close to the headboard. Thank God for my strong legs and ability to balance because it was not easy. I let him bury his face in my hole as I rode back and forth on his tongue clutching the headboard and desperately trying not to fall backward. I moaned and acted like it was the best rim job I had ever had, trying to reassure him he was doing a good job. I saw my reflection in an awful Egyptian painting on the wall in front of me, and I couldn't even make sense of what I was watching. I wanted to laugh at how ridiculous I must have looked, but I thought it would be more polite to continue acting like it was the best rim job ever.

"Fuck yeah, baby, that's awesome."

His tongue just stuck out as I did all the work, but I wanted to make him feel like a champ so I moaned and told him how great it felt as I held onto the headboard for dear life, my nails digging into the wood. It was at this point I thought I should definitely be given some kind of escort award because it felt like fucking Cirque du Soleil in his room. I was giving you theater, flexibility, and passion. Escort realness, Vegas style.

He wanted to fuck me, and thankfully getting him hard wasn't going to be a problem. I wrapped a condom around his dick, covered it in lube, and climbed on the bed. Again, this was going to require some balance and strength. I was unsure as to how I was going to do this, and I felt like I was looking at the periodic table of elements. I failed chemistry in high school, and I felt just as baffled now as I was figuring out a way to mount his dick and get fucked. As an escort, you have try to constantly look sexy, desirable, and "in the moment." You have to do this even if your partner is severely overweight or smells like he hasn't showered after a six-hour flight; if there's shit all over your dick, body, and bed from someone who didn't douche before sex; or when someone lathers an entire bottle of Astroglide lube all over your body and insists on rubbing himself on you for more than forty minutes. All of which has happened to me at least once.

Getting fucked by him ended up not being too difficult, although it took a lot of balance and put an incredible amount of strain on my legs. After riding him for a few minutes, I could tell he was close to cumming, so I climbed off and started to stroke his cock. He looked like he was enjoying it, but he also looked like he was in pain. I asked him if he was okay and he said yes, so I continued stroking, but harder and faster. I squirted some more lube on his dick to avoid chaffing and kept beating him off as he got closer and closer to cumming. Right before he did, he shouted, "I'm gonna cum!" I looked down, curious to see what his massive sperm build-up would look like. He began to shoot strings of cum everywhere, but then his cum went from a normal healthy white to a dark red. Blood was shooting out from his dick and all over his stomach, sheets, and my hands. *Oh, my God. I was not at all prepared for blood. What the fuck did I do to him?* I told myself to keep going and finish him off. The last thing I wanted to do was freak him out as he was losing his virginity.

After the blood stopped shooting from his dick and he stopped panting I asked, "Is everything okay?"

"Yeah, everything is fine. That was awesome! Thanks!"

"No problem." I paused and tried to sound completely normal and calm as I said, "There was a lot of blood in your cum, so I just want to be sure everything is okay and I didn't hurt you."

"Really, there was blood? I'm sorry," he sounded just as surprised as I was.

"I just want to be sure you're okay."

"Yes, I'm good. The blood was probably from having used catheters for so many years. I'm sorry."

"No need to apologize. I just want to be sure you're okay," I repeated.

"I'm good. Thanks." He smiled and I leaned down to give him a kiss on the lips.

I excused myself to wash my hands for at least three verses of "Happy Birthday." I knew he didn't have anything I should be worried about catching, and I didn't have any open wounds on my hands, but the whole experience of having blood shoot all over my hands was intense. I needed a few minutes to collect my thoughts before I returned to the bedroom.

After I cleaned up, I rejoined him. He asked if I would help him smoke a cigarette and he offered me one too.

"No, thank you. I'm headed to the gym soon, and smoking before a workout probably isn't the best thing." He laughed and I smiled at him as I pulled a Marlboro light out of the pack. A bedridden law student who can't move asked me to help him smoke a cigarette; that's kind of badass! He tells me his system for smoking: I put the cigarette in his mouth and he inhales, but when he blinks his eyes, it means he's had enough and I should remove the cigarette from his mouth. We did this for a few minutes, and he told me how happy he was with the whole encounter. He also mentioned how he couldn't wait to go back and tell all his friends he finally lost his virginity.

"You told everyone back home you were going to do this?"

"Yeah, sure. I told most of my friends and they think it's great," he said proudly.

I'm used to my clients being married or closeted or they've never been with a guy before. Some clients give me a fake name, call from a blocked number, and sometimes they buy a pay-by-the-minute phone to contact me. I was impressed by his "I don't give a fuck" attitude about contacting and having sex with an escort and then telling everyone about it.

"Cool," I said, proud to be this guy's first sexual experience. It seemed a little odd to think that all his friends, not to mention his male nurse, were anxiously waiting to hear about the escapade and ready to congratulate him. It was like he had just graduated, closed on a house, or had a given birth to a child.

He finished the cigarette and we chatted for a bit. I helped him drink his water from a bottle with a really long straw. I placed the straw in his mouth as I held the bottle and he would take a few sips, stop, and then take another few sips again. His nurse returned and very casually said hi and began making small-talk. I excused myself to shower and clean up. There was no awkwardness and no uncomfortable silences among the three of us. We all knew what had just happened for the past three hours, and that was that.

He said there was an envelope in the nightstand drawer with six hundred dollars in it. I removed it, put it in my pocket, and said my good-byes. I kissed him before I left, shook the nurse's hand, and was on my way to the gym.

Chapter Seven

One Man's Last Sexual Experience

A few days after my date with Craig at the Luxor, I got a phone call reminding me about a date I had set up with a man named Dale from Southern California. We had e-mailed back and forth, deciding on meeting in his room at Caesar's Palace on a Thursday night for two hours starting at 8 p.m. When I arrived I knocked on the door. A nice-looking man in a Hoveround scooter answered and greeted me warmly. I said hello, smiled back, and entered the room. I wasn't quite sure what to make of the scooter, because I see tons of people every day in casinos who can walk but use them when they come to Vegas. All the hotels and casinos on the strip look like they are close to each other, but they generally take a lot of time to get from one to another. Therefore, many people opt for a scooter, especially if they are not physically fit. Was this man one of them, or did he really need it full-time?

I realized this was a handicapped room because of the spacious layout and some of the machinery attached to the walls to assist him in getting around.

"So I guess you're wondering about the scooter," he said.

"Kind of. Is everything okay?"

"Yes. I actually suffer from multiple sclerosis, and over time I have lost most of the use of my legs and the rest of my body."

Seriously? Less than a week before, I was in a hotel room with Craig having an almost identical conversation. I had never before met anyone with advanced multiple sclerosis, and now I was about to have sex with my second in less than a week. Was the universe trying to tell me something?

As Dale spoke, his voice shook and he had a hard time getting out his words. At first, I thought maybe he had a learning disability or speech impediment because his sentences weren't making any sense. His voice quivered the entire time we spoke, and he couldn't formulate what he was thinking into complete sentences.

"Are you okay?" I asked.

"Yes, but to be honest, I'm really nervous, and I can't really say what I want because you're here. I've never done this and I can't think clearly."

"I see... don't worry about it. Just relax and take your time. We have two hours and I'm up for anything."

I could see that he was becoming a bit more at ease as we continued talking and he eventually began to calm down. He told me about his condition and how his body was fast deteriorating. He called me because he found me attractive and wanted to have a sexual experience while he still had some mobility left in his body. He was worried that in the next four to six months he would lose the use of his entire body and this was going to be the last experience before he was completely immobile.

This information took a lot to process. A few days earlier, I had a twenty-eight-year-old virgin who couldn't move asking me to be his first sexual experience, and now I had a middle-aged man in a scooter asking me to be his last sexual partner. Again, I felt tiny, insignificant, and completely humble. This was all a lot of pressure and hard to process. What could I possibly do to fulfill this man's expectations for a final sexual experience? I began to get more nervous and a little worried. I looked at the clock and noticed that we had been speaking for more than an hour. If we were going to try anything, we had to move quickly. I had no idea if I was going to be doing all the work like when Craig and I had sex, or if he was going to be able to do some as well.

I said we should probably get started, and he laughed, apologizing for talking too much.

"No worries. How about next time we meet I bring you some Xanax and we can have a drink to calm your nerves?" He laughed and agreed.

I excused myself to go to the bathroom and he began hoisting himself out of the scooter and onto the bed. This was quite a process to watch. I asked if I could help or if he needed me to do anything, but he said he was fine. I couldn't believe this man went through this every time he got in or out of bed and my respect for him grew. I was impressed that Dale was able to make this journey to Las Vegas alone, able to figure out a way to get around and take care of himself with such limited mobility.

I came out of the bathroom and once again glanced at the clock. I had another appointment directly after Dale with a regular client named Rodney. I didn't want Dale to sense that I was rushing things, but I wanted to be sure I had enough to time to give both guys the attention they expected and were paying for. I had no idea how Dale and I were going to do anything in less than forty minutes that would make this a memorable experience for him.

The rest of our time together is a blur now. We experimented with making out, body contact, oral sex, and I was able to fuck him for a little while. It was difficult topping him since he couldn't move much of his lower body, but we somehow made it work for a few minutes. He basically lied there on his side with his ass close to the edge while I stood on the floor, stuck my dick in him, and fucked him. It was an awkward position, and I wasn't sure if he was getting anything out of it, but I kept going and tried to focus on keeping my dick hard. Plus, it was getting closer and closer to the two-hour mark, and I had to leave on time to meet Rodney at The M Resort.

I asked him if he could cum, but he said he didn't know if it was going to happen anytime soon. I apologized and told him I had to get going to meet friends. He understood and apologized for everything. I told him there was nothing to apologize for, that I was just sorry the session turned out the way it had. I cleaned up and gathered my stuff. I genuinely felt bad that this experience probably wasn't everything he had fantasized about, or hoped for, but duty called and I had to run. We made small-talk as I got dressed, and we agreed to keep in touch. He told me he would try his best to make another trip to Las Vegas in the next few months.

"Next time we meet," I said, "we'll do less talking and more fucking." He laughed and I winked and smiled at him. He said there was an envelope in the dresser drawer with six hundred dollars in it. I took it out, put it in my pocket, and said my good-byes, giving him a hug and a kiss before I left.

I left Caesars Palace and was on my way to The M Resort on South Las Vegas Boulevard, the outskirts of the city. I knew I had to book it to make it on time. As I left the hotel, Rodney texted me to see if I was on my way. I responded that I was, and he asked if it was cool for another escort to join us. This could either be really good or really bad. I always want to know who the other guy was, because after a few years of working in this industry, you learn there are a lot of guys that also do this who you want to steer clear of. Some of the guys were known to be heavy drug users, some had set up fake profiles online, and some had reputations of being egotistical assholes you try to avoid at all costs. Rodney replied, "It's another dude I hire out for massage." Most of the escorts I knew of in the city were escorts only, so I assumed I didn't know who the other guy was and just planned on being surprised. But the more I thought about it, the more paranoid I became. Sometimes it's better to go into a meeting with a client knowing very little about the situation or the others involved.

I had met Rodney in January 2011 during CES, the huge electronics convention held annually in Las Vegas that draws over one hundred thousand visitors. My first meeting with him was a blur, because as I was parking the car at the hotel, I got a phone call from Rick Thomas, my boss and star of the show I was in at the time, who called to fire me. Apparently, one of his longtime dancers—and old friend—had moved back to Vegas and wanted his job back. He said he would keep me in his show as an understudy, or I could leave the show on my own accord, but the full-time position was going back to his previous employee because they had an "agreement." Rick told me, "I'm really sorry about this Christopher, but this is how show business works." I wanted to tell him to go fuck himself, but I was speechless. I had no contract with the production company who produced the show, and I had no legal grounds to stand on, so basically I was fucked and not in a good way. Rick asked me how I wanted to handle the situation. Furious and upset, I remained silent for a few seconds before finally telling him I couldn't make a decision right then because I was in the middle of something. I hung up, and needless to say, my first meeting with Rodney was overshadowed by this drama. Surprisingly, we did have good sexual chemistry and I found him to be really sexy.

Rodney and I met several times over the next year, but we never had any anal penetration and only rarely had any oral sex. He really got into hand-jobs, light kissing, watching me touch his body in a full-length mirror, and pressing my naked body against his from behind. Over time, he began to share with me his sexual fantasies, and we began to experiment with various taboo scenarios he would fantasize about. Most involved him being sexually molested by an older male or molesting me. He opened up to me during our first visit and told me he had been sexually abused as a kid, but he loved it and still fantasized about it every day. This screamed dysfunctional to me, but who was I to judge? Besides, he was nice, good-looking, and funny. The sessions were quick, and I didn't even have to douche to meet him! He was what I'd like to think of as an ideal client, minus the disturbing childhood molestation scenarios he would ask me to re-create with him.

I made my way to his room, knocked, and he answered from behind the door to let me in. Already naked, he smiled, put his finger to his mouth, and said, "Shhhhhhhhh." He pointed to the other escort, sitting on the bed naked and talking on the phone to someone about driving to LA the next day and agreeing on a time to meet up.

I looked at Rodney and in a very serious tone whispered, "Don't tell me what to fucking do." He looked confused and I just smiled at him and said, "I'm just fucking with you," before giving him a hug. We had known each other long enough now that we could joke around and tease each other and have a good time.

He told me how good I looked and how happy he was I was able to make it. I set my stuff down on the dresser, and Rodney started to undress me immediately, but I stopped him to excuse myself to go to the bathroom. I took a piss and heard the two guys talking about something. I came out of the bathroom to see Rodney lying on the bed and the other guy standing above him naked. The other escort was tall, very white, soft around the middle, had an average body—at best—and looked uninteresting from head to toe. Perfect, he was definitely not my type in the least bit, and there was absolutely no competition between us who would be the hotter escort for the night. I won just by showing up.

"Should I even bother with introductions?" Rodney asked, and the other guy and I just looked at each other.

"Sure," I said as I began to undress.

"This is Chad. He's straight and gives me the best hand-jobs."

63

Straight? Oh, that's perfect, I thought sarcastically. Working with straight guys—like in the porn industry—was a pet peeve of mine. They rarely kiss, rim, or suck dick; there's no connection or chemistry; and they rarely—if ever—can get or maintain an erection. So basically, I was left doing all the work as they watched the clock with a slight uneasy look on their face. It almost looked as if they were thinking, "I can't believe I'm letting some dude suck my cock for cash. Fuck my life." I found that guys who were only gay-for-pay were in it for the quick and easy money, and sometimes they worked my last nerve. Chad wasn't even all that cute, at least in my opinion, and he looked like he hadn't stepped in a gym for a few years. I guess it didn't matter what I thought, because Rodney seemed to really like him. I had no interest in getting to know him or playing with him, even if Rodney asked. I'm not sure what it is about straight escorts, but clients seem to love them. It's almost as if because the clients have no chance of ever getting them—other than by paying them—so it was a huge turn-on for them. Talk about self-loathing homosexuals. The clients loved the challenge, and it was almost as if these guys not giving "it" up would just keep these men coming back for more. It was like the straight escorts were playing these men like I had seen women play the men who came into strip clubs. It was a game and they were winning. I, on other hand, give it all away and at times still felt like I was struggling just to keep the clients I had. Maybe I should work on being more butch or re-create myself as a gay-for-pay escort—but I'm not too sure many people would really buy that.

Rodney told Chad, "Christopher and I get into role playing and he's the best at it." That's not something I would put under special skills on a résumé, but he was right. I was pretty good at it and could get into it depending on the scenario or the situation. I smiled and dropped all my clothes on the floor, but then pick them up and fold them to put on the dresser. Hotel rooms are filthy, and the last thing I want is my underwear and clean shirt lying on the floor that you know at least one tourist has either had sex on or threw up on.

Rodney asked me to lie next to him as Chad poured baby oil on his body and lathered him up. I wasn't even sure what Chad was doing, or if it was enjoyable for Rodney. It just looked like he was squirting baby oil on his hands and rubbing it into Rodney's body like you would see two "straight dudes" applying sunblock on each other at the beach. He looked uneasy and completely uncomfortable. I began to wonder if there would be a mortified look on this straight guy's face when Rodney began acting like an eleven-year-old boy asking me to play with his "pee pee."

"I want Chad to massage me, and I want you to lie next to me, Christopher, and talk dirty to me." All of a sudden, I began to feel self-conscious about the stuff Rodney wanted me to say. I felt like I would be judged if I delved right into the same scenarios we usually got into. I felt like I'd start talking dirty and this straight guy would get freaked out more than he already was. I had no shame doing what I was doing, but I guess even I would think it was a little odd hearing it for the first time. I told myself to get over it and just start acting like the little boy Rodney wanted me to be, because that was the reason Rodney was paying me to be there.

Rodney liked to start with me being a little twelve-year-old boy climbing into bed with his Daddy, and he began to touching me. I'm not sure who had molested Rodney or if it had been incest, but he loved to pretend to be a father molesting his son. The scenarios were hard to get into at first, because it felt like I was taking part in something that was even pushing my sexual limits. Sex with minors was not something I fantasized about or had any desire to do, but I came to realize that many guys I met either had fantasies about molesting a little boy, or being the boy that was being taken advantage of. Right away, Rodney started treating me like a perverted preteen wanting his father to take advantage of him. I pretended to get into it and acted like I didn't want it but secretly did. Obviously, I was playing the role of the little boy getting taken advantage of, and Rodney loved it. Chad continued to awkwardly touch Rodney's body and occasionally stroke his cock.

Chad's uncut dick was completely flaccid. He just knelt next to Rodney, looking very uneasy as he tried his best not to make eye contact with either one of us.

"You like climbing into bed with your Daddy and stroking his big, fat cock?" Rodney asked me.

"Yes, Daddy, you know I do. It feels so good."

"I want you to do this every night. Okay, Christopher?"

"But what if we get caught?" I asked.

"We won't, because we'll be very quiet and not tell anyone. Will you tell anyone?"

"No, Daddy, I won't, but what if someone hears us?"

"Shhh... nobody will hear us if you're quiet. Don't say anything and keep touching Daddy's big cock, okay?"

"Okay, Daddy, but why is it so big?" I asked. I knew he loved to hear any reference to his "big dick." It drove him absolutely crazy and made him even harder. His eyes got so big they looked like they were going to pop out of his head.

"It's big because you turn me on so much, boy. You like turning Daddy on, Christopher?"

"Yes, Daddy, I do. I like to make Daddy feel good."

"Fuck yeah, that's fucking hot," he whispered in my ear. He then told us to switch positions, and Chad and I traded spots. I went on the other side and rubbed Rodney's body with baby oil, and Rodney put Chad's flaccid, uncut, pierced dick in his mouth and forced himself to gag on it.

Sometimes, when I am working with another escort, I like to make eye contact with him so we can look at each other, smile, and roll our eyes as if to say, "Can you believe we're doing this?" With Chad, I had no connection and would have preferred he wasn't even in the room. He was doing a fraction of what I was doing, his body looked like shit, and he was probably getting paid the same. Why do I even bother working so hard in this industry? I look at guys like Chad and I'm annoyed with myself for taking my work so seriously. Obviously guys like Chad don't, and he probably was doing pretty well for himself.

We went on like this for about twenty minutes, switching back and forth. Finally, Rodney stood up and said, "Okay, let's go stand in front of the mirror like we usually do, Christopher. You know I like that." He stopped and looked at Chad and said, "Dude, you're not even hard!"

Chad laughed nervously and replied, "Uh, I know. I think it's because of stage fright."

"Bullshit," I snapped. I was not there to make friends and this kid annoyed me. I tried my best to make sure Chad felt uncomfortable at this point so Rodney would let him leave and we could wrap this session up. I knew what worked for him, and this other escort was really cramping my style and getting in the way of what we usually do. I stood behind Rodney, pressed my body against him, and embraced him. Chad just stood there and kind of rubbed Rodney's stomach and stroked his dick.

"Christopher, stroke Chad's cock and let me watch in the mirror." I began to stroke Chad, and I had to admit his dick felt pretty good. I wished this kid was more into this, because he had a nice uncut dick, and I could probably give him better head than his girlfriend. Surprisingly, Chad began to get hard, and maybe I was on to something and he wasn't so straight after all.

Rodney interrupted us and said, "Okay, guys, let's go back to the bed. Chad, dude, you're hard now!"

He laughed nervously and said, "Yeah, I know."

"Is this your first three-way, Chad?" Rodney wondered out loud.

"With two guys, yeah."

"Yeah, me too," I said to Rodney.

"Really?" Rodney asked.

"Yeah, my first three-way this week." I smiled and winked at Rodney, who laughed hard.

We climbed back into bed and Rodney instructed me to lay down next to him and Chad to keep stroking his dick. He asked me to put a finger in his ass and talk dirty to him. Going for the baby oil, I noticed the greasy handprints on the headboard and bedspread. I always felt bad for the cleaning ladies who worked in these hotels because I envision them trying to scrub out oil stains and silicone lube out of the bedspreads, pillows, walls, and headboards that my clients and I have ruined over the years. I put some oil on my index finger to lube it up and slowly started rubbing Rodney's taint, moving in closer toward his hole.

"Fuck yeah, Christopher. You like Daddy's hole?"

"Daddy, you know I love your hole." I say.

"Fuck yeah! Daddy, I love it when you play with my hole," said Rodney. He loved to switch roles halfway through, so suddenly he became the little boy getting molested. It confused me at first, but I got used to going from being a small boy being molested to the child molester himself.

"I know you do, son. You like it when Daddy comes in your room and starts touching you?"

"Yes, Daddy, but what if Mommy comes in?" he asked.

"She won't come in if you're quiet. Just be quiet and we'll be fine," I said. As I pushed my finger in deeper and deeper, his eyes opened wider and wider. He began to whimper and I said, "Be quiet before your mother comes in." As he lay back down, I glanced out of the corner of my eye to see Chad looking incredibly uncomfortable and uneasy. It took me awhile to feel okay with saying this stuff, or hearing it, but I finally realized it was this guy's fantasy and I wasn't there to judge or figure out why he liked what he liked. As with many other situations with clients, I needed to put my personal opinions aside and do what I get paid to do.

"Fuck, guys, I love having you both here stroking my dick. I love when you switch roles, Christopher. It drives me crazy."

"I know you do, son," I said and smiled at him.

"Okay, I'm really close to cumming, guys. What time do you have to leave Chad?"

"Uh, in like ten minutes, I think."

"Okay, perfect. Christopher, come lie down here on my left side, and, Chad, come lie on the other side. I'm going turn on my favorite porn and jerk off." He retrieved the iPad from next to the bed and turned on a porn with two guys. One of them was a hot, hairy, muscled daddy, and the other was a younger fit guy in a black mask.

"This is the hottest scene ever. This masked guy is going to stroke this guy off and call him daddy. Okay, guys, touch my body, and I'm going to jerk off." He began to switch off between masturbating, watching the porn, and closing his eyes. He did this for a few minutes and edged himself closer and closer to a climax.

"Oh, fuck yeah." He turned to the porn and said, "That little boy is going to make him cum. He's doing it now. Watch him, he calls him daddy as he strokes his cock." So we all watched the beefy hairy dude in the scene shoot his load.

"Oh my God, you guys, I'm gonna cum," and he did something I had never seen him do before. He took a giant deep breath and held it in. He continued stroking his cock for about ten seconds and shook his head back and forth like he was being choked. His face started turned purple, and he finally shot a load all over himself. After he came, he convulsed back and forth, gasping for air. I realized I was witnessing autoerotic asphyxiation for the first time. Wow, that was a new one.

We all lay together for a few minutes and Rodney continued to shake a little from the aftershock of the orgasm and loss of air. Chad got up to grab a towel, and I got up to stretch my legs.

"There are no more towels," Rodney said. "My roommate and I used them up."

"You have someone staying in here with you?" I asked.

"Yeah, some straight guy I work with." I looked around the room and saw towels everywhere, clothes on the floor, oily handprints on the headboard and on the comforter. *Poor roommate*, I thought. *I wonder if he has any idea what is going on in his room?*

I got up to shower, even though there were no towels. I spotted a small hand towel and figured that was good enough. There was no way I was leaving the hotel all greased up in baby oil and smelling like sweat. I would drip dry if I had to. I rinsed off in the shower and watched as Chad gathered his stuff together. I was trying to avoid an awkward good-bye, so I was happy to see him leave before I had finished rinsing off. I stepped out of the shower and dried off with the small hand towel and watched Rodney in his boxers wash up in the sink, taking a whore's bath with a used face cloth.

"So, dude, I totally met a guy," Rodney told me excitedly.

"Really? Who is he?"

"He's this twenty-one-year-old. He's so fucking hot, and can you believe we spent a whole week together? All he wanted to do was fuck the entire time, and I couldn't even keep up with him. He'd beg for it like three to four times a day, and I'd say I can't, but of course, I'd wait like five minutes, then we'd start fucking. It was so hot."

"That's great. Who is he? Where'd you meet?"

"We met on seekingmillionaire.com."

"Is that anything like seekingarrangement.com?"

"Yeah, it's a sister site," he informed me.

"I set up a profile on Seeking Arrangement after someone told me about it, but it seemed like a lot of bullshit to put up with."

"Yeah, it is, but I put my ad on this other site, and I clearly said in my ad that I didn't want a gold digger. I wanted a young guy genuinely interested in older men."

"I see. That's pretty cool," I said, although I was wondering what the chances were of a young guy looking for an older man on a site called Seeking a Millionaire not being a gold digger. Good luck, Rodney, because I don't think such a guy really exists.

"Yeah, it was amazing. I even told him I love him."

"Really? That's pretty intense."

"It is, but I really think I do."

"What about your wife, though? And how the hell did you get away from her for a week without her becoming suspicious?"

"I go away for a week by myself every year, and I met this guy online, so I flew out and stayed in Denver for a few days, and we spent the whole time together. I think I'm going to leave my wife."

"Are you serious?" I asked. To me this whole scenario had disaster written all over it.

"Yeah, I'm done. I don't want to do this anymore."

"I totally understand, but are you leaving her and your family to be with this kid?" I asked.

"Kind of, but I know the marriage isn't working anymore. We haven't had sex in over a year, and all we do is fight. I'll give her half of everything and pay her alimony until my twelve-year-old girl graduates high school, and I don't care. I know she's going to take me to the cleaners, and I'm basically screwed."

"Just be careful with this young kid. If something goes wrong, he could manipulate the situation and blackmail you. I've seen this happen with other guys and I would be wary of trusting such a young kid no matter what he says. Just stay guarded with what information you tell him. If he feels like you've screwed him, he could fuck you over royally." I don't know who I thought I was to be giving Rodney advice, but it just seemed like he could potentially be setting himself up for a huge disaster. I cared about him and have seen this kind of thing happen to a lot of men, but I didn't think it was registering with Rodney. He was about to leave his wife, burst out of the closet, and marry his little "Anna Nicole Smith Boy Toy."

"Yeah, I know that kind of shit happens. Didn't something happen like that with an escort in Las Vegas?"

"Did it?" I asked.

"Yeah, it was all over the news. When I saw it on TV, I thought they were talking about you. Apparently, some escort blackmailed and totally screwed over this New Jersey politician."

"I haven't heard anything about it. That's crazy, but it wasn't me. I like being personable with my clients and getting to know them, but I learned a long time ago to keep my professional life and personal life separate. I have no interest in blackmailing clients, or even knowing more about them then they care to share. It just gets too complicated on both ends."

"True, but I feel like it's different with this kid. We spent the entire night spooning and cuddling and it felt great. We literally didn't leave each other's arms the entire night."

It obviously sounded like he was in a place where he was yearning for close physical contact with a man. He had been starved of it his whole life and had been looking for it which explains the crazy fucked-up role-play situations we explored. Like other gay kids growing up, he had been looking for intimacy with another male and he ended up finding it in the arms of a child molester. He seemed like a smart enough man to know molesting a child was wrong, but you could tell his being molested as a young boy had shaped him and his sexuality for the rest of his life. I remember feeling the same way as a young kid, yearning for attention from another man that wasn't rejection or teasing like what I endured every day. I realize this probably sounds unhealthy and a little bit fucked up, but I even remember thinking being molested by an older man might have been a way to help ease the pain of not having any intimacy at all. As a kid, I didn't fully understand what sexual abuse involved, but I was in desperate need of some type of love and affirmation from a male and thought that was how you could get it. Hearing Rodney talk and spending time with him brought up some of my own unresolved stuff from my past and forced me to look at some issues I forgot existed.

I probably wouldn't see Rodney for a few months, and I was anxious to learn how everything unfolded for him. He told me his goal was to just get through Christmas, and then he would begin the necessary steps to get the divorce. He didn't want to be the asshole that left his family before Christmas, so he would wait until it was the New Year to start the process.

I wished him luck, gave him a hug, and was on my way.

Chapter Eight

Change Your Shirt and Walk Around the Room.

I received an e-mail from a man named Jimmy from New York saying he was visiting Las Vegas again and wanted to see me. He said he had seen me once before and would like to book another three-hour session and asked what the cost would be. I asked where I saw him before, and he replied he met me at the Wynn Resort with another well-known escort named Peter two years earlier. He asked if I remembered who he was, and I responded back with "Of course."

It made me laugh when clients asked if I remember them, because all it really takes is for someone to tell me when and where I saw them before and one other thing about our meeting, and I can generally remember everything about our time together. Usually, all they had to say was what they did for a living, where they were from, or what weird or different thing we did together, whether it be piss, role play, verbal abuse, and so on.

I remembered my meeting with Jimmy vividly. We had met in a huge suite at his hotel in February 2010, and I was anxious to see if this meeting would be like the last. It had been strange, to say the least, and while we didn't have sex or doing anything physical with each other, it was definitely memorable.

I got to the meeting a few minutes late because first I slept through my alarm and then I had to meet a friend to pick up a costume I was wearing for Halloween, which was in two days. I was already annoyed because I wasn't able to eat a big breakfast—which I have to do every day—drink my coffee, and go to the bathroom and douche. Whether or not I was going to be fucked by a client or for a porn shoot, I needed to be sure I was completely cleaned out and my insides felt empty. The last thing I want is for there to be a mess and have to excuse myself to go clean up. This only takes up time for both parties, is not the most pleasant smell client is trying to get "in the mood," and is somewhat embarrassing.

Jimmy was staying at the Wynn Resort again. When I arrived, he opened the door and was waiting with an escort I knew named Nick. He and I had become friends over the past few years, co-workers, and occasional fuck buddies. Clients liked to see us together because we kind of had this little brother–big brother thing going on. We had similar body types and were both blond with blue eyes, but the main difference was that he's about five foot five, and I am six foot one.

Nick was already shirtless and barefoot, which probably meant they had already begun. There was a pile of T-shirts, polo shirts, and ball caps on the dresser, and Jimmy was naked from the waist below with a raging hard-on and a bottle of KY in his hand. Obviously, he was ready to go.

Jimmy went to sit on a chair in the living room in front of a huge set of windows overlooking the Las Vegas Strip. It was a beautiful, sunny fall day in October and I was a little annoyed I was missing the cool weather outside. It felt like one of those days where you want to put on a warm sweater, grab a coffee from Starbucks, and head to the park. Vegas had very few sunny days with mild weather, so when it was nice the locals would eat it up.

The room was gorgeous and beautifully decorated. The Wynn and the Encore Hotel (the newest Wynn property) were two of the nicest places to stay in Las Vegas. I saw a lot of clients there and generally the ones I saw always had a lot of money and were very generous. The name "Steve Wynn" meant one thing in Vegas, which was class. Not too sure if the activities I was about to partake in were apart of Steve Wynn's vision for his hotels, but I'm sure he wouldn't care as long as he was making money. In Vegas, like anywhere, we all had our price and nobody really cared what anybody else was doing as long as their own needs were being met.

Jimmy was sitting there quietly, just looking at both of us, stroking his dick. "Nick, come sit on my knee and play with my nipples. Christopher, take your shirt off and walk around the room," he instructed. It looked like we were going to be doing the exact same scenario as I had done with him before. None of it really bothered me, but it was very different from what I was used to. It could be confusing for a first-timer taking part in the session.

I took off my shirt and threw it on the sofa, then began to pace the room.

"You like that don't you, Nick? You're a little pretty boy and I love your chest. You have the most amazing body. You are so fucking beautiful, and I can't stand it. Christopher, isn't he beautiful?" he asked me.

"Yes, he is," I answered.

"Christopher, take off your pants, underwear, shoes, and socks and stand in front of me." I did as I was told and stood in front of them both. "Oh, my God... Christopher, you are so fucking gorgeous. Isn't he gorgeous, Nick?"

"Yes, he is," Nick shyly answered as he looked around the room. I had already been through this with Jimmy, so it wasn't new to me, but I remember the first time I met him I found the whole thing to be awkward and unlike anything I have ever done. Jimmy didn't really do anything with us, instead he just brought in a pile of T-shirts, polo shirts, and ball caps and had us constantly taking off clothes and changing into new things.

"Nick, get up and take everything off. Walk around the room and go stand at that front window." Nick looked confused and embarrassed, but he did as he was told. I just stood in front of him naked, ready to follow my next direction.

"Christopher, come over here, sit on my lap, and play with my nipples." I did as I was told and he continued to stroke his cock. His dick was kind of small, mainly because it was surrounded by his belly and covered in long wiry pubic hairs. I really didn't care what this guy wanted, and I was fine with everything, as long as he didn't want me to suck his dick. I've sucked a lot of cock in my lifetime and I usually loved doing it, but the hardest thing for me was sucking dick covered in an enormous belly and pubic hair. The stench from a crotch like that could be overpowering and the smell would sometimes linger in your nose for hours, sometimes days, afterward.

"I'm a recovering alcoholic and I don't use drugs, so getting a massage really opens my mind and helps me relax. Will you rub my shoulders, Christopher?" I do so willingly as I try to balance myself my six-foot-one frame and two-hundred-pound body on his knee.

"Jesus, Christopher... that's amazing," he said. "Nick, go put on your jeans, shoes, hat, and a different shirt. Christopher, go put some pants on and walk around." We both did as we were told, and after Nick got dressed, Jimmy told us to make out. We approached each other and did so willingly. Having another escort there to fool around with always helps make the time go by faster, and we were both thankful the other one was there. It was also comforting when it was someone you knew and had good chemistry with. It made the whole process a little more fun and enjoyable.

"Okay, that's enough. Nick, take off your shirt, put it in your back pocket, and stand in front of me. Christopher, get dressed in another polo shirt, put on a ball cap, and walk around. Nick, sit on my lap and play with my nipples again."

Again, I got dressed in yet another outfit from the pile of clothes he brought and began to walk around.

"All right, Nick, get up and go make out with Christopher." Again, we did as we were told. "Okay, Christopher, come over here and rub my shoulders." I left Nick to go rub his shoulders. He moaned and smileed like it was the best feeling he had ever had. This man was seriously loving this and totally getting off. "Oh, my God, this is amazing." Nick continued to walk around the room, and I continued to rub Jimmy's shoulders.

"Look at Nick... isn't he gorgeous?" he asked me.

I nodded and said, "Yes, he is."

"I love to watch beautiful young guys like you two... walking around, taking your shirts off, and being sexy. You both are so fucking hot, it drives me crazy and I can't even deal with it. I love pretty boys with hot fucking bodies and it drives me insane to know I can never have either one of you. The only way a gross guy like me could get a guy like you is to pay for it, and that's fucking hot." He let out a scream and said, "Wow... okay, I need to stop for a second." Apparently, our "hotness" and presence was too much for him, and he needed a break. Neither one of us had done anything, except play with his nipples over his T-shirt, give him a neck rub, get naked, and make out with each other, but the intensity of it all was too much for Jimmy. As he excused himself and went to the bathroom, I looked at Nick.

"How's it going?" I asked.

He smiled and said, "Good, I'm kind of tired and totally hungry. I really wanted to stop at Starbucks and get some food but the line was so long."

"I know," I replied. " I woke up late and had no time to eat."

We both rolled our eyes and half smiled at each other. I asked him, "So this stuff is pretty interesting, isn't it?"

He laughed quietly and said, "Yeah right... really, uh, interesting." I guess you could say this was our version of escorting water-cooler chat.

Jimmy returned with a small Bose speaker and an iPod.

"This stuff we're doing really helps me work through my issues from my past. I remember coming out of the closet in the '80s and being really young and fat, and sitting in bars watching guys like you two knowing I could never have them. You guys probably think I'm crazy, and this stuff is kind of different, but I really get off on it." Nick was quiet, but I reassured the man that it was not a problem and we were cool with whatever he wanted to get into. "You're going to have to excuse my bad taste in music, but I wanna put on some music from the '80s to help bring back some memories. It's all very New York late 1970s and early 1980s"

"Yeah, that's cool... do what you gotta do," I told him.

He put on some disco music and sat back down on the chair. He squeezed a giant gob of KY jelly into his hand and began jerking off again. He spit on his hand to make it even wetter, and a look of satisfaction came over his face as he slipped back into his relaxed state of mind. Jimmy seemed like a really nice guy, but he looked like a dirty old man stroking his cock and moaning in the chair. I guess he had no other way of getting laid unless he paid for it, but that was probably why he was so turned on by the scenario we were creating for him. Money is power and this man knew without his cash, he had no chance of being with hot young men. Aside from getting dressed and undressed, standing around naked, playing with his nipples, and occasionally Nick and me kissing each other, there was really no sex going on between anyone.

He told Nick to circulate the room, and then told me to sit back down on his knee and rub his shoulders again. I squatted my body back on his knee without putting my full weight on him and tried not to crush him. Doing this was killing my quads, and I was feeling the pain from my leg work-out from the previous day at the gym.

"Yeah, that's fucking awesome. It makes me feel really good. You like to make me feel good?"

I nodded in agreement as I made direct eye contact with him. I could tell this guy was getting intense and I wanted to show him that I was equally intense and not fucking around with him. Nick seemed a little freaked out by the incident, but I have seen weirder behavior and I figured to make the three hours go by quicker and at least make it seem interesting, I should engage him and get into it as much as I could. I was not into whatever this guy was doing, but I always liked to test my boundaries and see how far I could go when faced with new or odd situations with clients.

Continuing to hold the direct eye contact with me, he asked, "You wanna be my boy?"

"Uh-huh," I answered.

"You been a good boy for me?"

"You know I have. I've always been your good little boy."

"Oh, man, that's awesome. I love hearing that. " He closed his eyes and dropped his head into a state of relaxation. I continued rubbing his shoulders, and Nick was still wandering around the room.

"Nick, I want you to stop, turn around, and look out the window. Christopher, I want you to get off me and start walking around the room."

I did as I was told, not sure what it was that turned him on about seeing two guys wandering around a hotel room, but he was loving every minute of it.

"Okay, Christopher. Take off your shirt and keep walking around. Nick, get naked and come stand directly in front of me." We did as we were told for the next few minutes.

"You have a nice ass, Nick."

"Thanks," he answered innocently.

"You want Christopher to fuck that ass?"

Nick's eyes opened as he perked up and said, "Yes, I do."

"Christopher, take off your jeans. Come over here, bend Nick over the table, and fuck his ass."

78

I took off my jeans and started stroking my dick to get it hard. I'm already semi hard, and the Viagra began to kick in. I took a condom out of my bag as well as the lube, bent Nick over the dining room table, and lubed up his hole. Nick eagerly bent over and got ready to take my rock-hard dick. You could tell this was probably going to be the highlight of Nick's morning, and I was happy to give it to him. Nick has always been an eager bottom when we've been together sexually and he can always take a good pounding, even though I remembered I had made his ass bleed a few times. I began fucking him and he moaned as I went in and out of his tight pink hole. We fuck for about two minutes, and then Jimmy stopped us and told us to go into the other room. Jimmy didn't have much interest in having sex with us or seeing us have sex. The meeting was not about that; instead it was about changing outfits, walking around, and reminding him of the years he spent as a self-loathing man coming out of the closet. To Jimmy, this scenario and experience were more pleasurable than actual sex.

We went into the bedroom and he asked me to shut the blinds. As I did so, Jimmy took a seat in the chair next to the window. Nick walked into the room a minute later, still naked, and took a sip of water from his bottle.

"Christopher, come sit back down on my knee, and, Nick, shut the door and walk around the room." By this point, the drapes were closed, the bedroom door was shut, and there was hardly any light in the room. We could still see the glaring sunlight creep in underneath the drapes, but it was pretty dark.

"Nick, put your jeans back on and climb on top of the bed and face the window. Christopher, can you keep rubbing my neck?" We did as we were told for the next few minutes until he instructed us to switch positions. I lifted myself off Jimmy's knee, and Nick climbed down from the bed and onto Jimmy. I hoisted myself on top of the beautifully made queen-size bed and faced the window. I stood up there fighting yawns as Nick stroked Jimmy's nipples and he continued to edge his dick closer to an orgasm. We did this for a few minutes, and I seriously began to think I was going to fall asleep standing there in the completely silent and dark room.

"Let's move this back into the living room," Jimmy said, and Nick climbed off and I stepped down from the bed. I looked at the alarm next to the bed and saw we had already been going at it for close to two hours.

It hadn't seemed that long, but it surprised me that we had basically been doing nothing except walking around, standing, changing clothes, sitting on his knee, pinching his nipples, and occasionally massaging his neck. This was definitely one of the strangest yet easiest gigs I have ever had to do as an escort.

I excused myself to use the bathroom as they made their way to the living room. I took a few minutes for myself in there to use the toilet, splash some cold water on my face, and breathe for a few minutes. I glanced into the mirror and I thought I looked like shit. I barely got any sleep the night before and I didn't feel my best. I knew this was an easy gig, but I was ready for it to be done with so I could go home and get in a catnap before I hit the gym.

I came out of the bathroom to see Nick packing up his stuff and getting ready to leave about halfway through the appointment. Jimmy had told me in the e-mail he sent a few weeks back that he would usually ask one of the escorts to leave so he could have some one-on-one time with the other guy. I guess I was the other guy chosen to stay behind. He handed Nick his money and thanked him for making time to see him. Nick smiled, thanked him, and gave him a hug, then walked over to me, hugged me, and we said our good-byes. Since it was Halloween weekend, I told him I was sure we'd be seeing each other out at the clubs. He checked for his keys, wallet, and phone and was on his way out.

After Jimmy closed the door behind Nick, he walked over to the iPod and chose a new song. I didn't recognize any of the music, but it was fun and I liked the disco beat it had. I wasn't around the gay clubs in NYC in the '70s and '80s, but I'm sure this is what they all played.

He sat back down on a chair and asked me to put on a ball cap and sit on his knee and gently pinch his nipples. I found the cap he brought and squeezed it on my head. My head was bigger than most guys, and I had a hard time finding hats, but I managed to squeeze my head into the ones he brought.

"Nick is a nice kid," he said, "but I don't know if he was really into what we were doing."

"Yeah, he seemed a little unsure about it, but he's a good guy."

"Really?"

"Yeah, I've known him for a while and I really like him." I smiled at Jimmy, and he asked me to pinch a little harder on his nipples.

"Too hard," he said. "I like it a little hard but not too much. A little more gentle." He closed his eyes, laid his head back, and began to relax again. "That's it... oh, my God that feels so good."

"You like that?" I asked

"Oh, yeah. It feels great."

"You like it when I pinch your nips for you?"

"Oh, man... yeah. I'm a dirty motherfucker. I fucking love it."

"You're a dirty perverted fucker aren't you?" I asked.

"Oh, yeah, man. I'm fucking disgusting."

"You're disgusting, you perverted fuck?" I asked.

"I'm so fucking disgusting, Chris. Tell me how disgusting I am... tell me," he commanded.

"You're so fucking gross and disgusting; I can't even stand looking at you."

"Oh, fuck yeah," he moaned.

"You fucking like it when a hot guy comes to your room and pinches your nipples, you perverted fucker?" I asked, and we continued this dialogue of utter humiliation and he ate it up.

"I fucking love it. I'm so fucking disgusting and gross. I fucking need hot guys like you to come over here and make me feel like a total pig."

"That's because you are total pig. You're a disgusting, gross, perverted twisted, fucking pig." This turned him on even more and he closed his eyes, threw his head back, and began stroking his cock harder and faster.

"Fuck, yeah. You know I am. Okay... get up and stand over there."

I did as I was told and stood across from him, naked and wearing a hat. I looked at him and said, "You are such a disgusting fucking faggot. You are so fucking gross, sitting there stroking your dick. You're fucking pathetic..." And at that moment he made direct eye contact with me, sent out a loud groan, and I saw cum shoot out of his dick and fly at least five feet across the room and all over the floor. I guess humiliating him and degrading him will do the trick and make him cum. I've heard of guys getting off on this, but this was my first time seeing a guy so turned on by me calling him such vile things.

There was silence in the room, and after a few moments, I offered to get him a towel. He said sure and thanked me. I walked to the bathroom and grabbed a small hand towel and ran it under warm water. I brought it to him, and he began to clean up and then put on some loose gym shorts. We made small-talk, and he told me of his travel plans. He asked me if I had any travel plans, and I told him I was headed to New York next week. He asked me if I knew a guy named Javier out there who hosts these nights at various bars in New York City where he hires strippers. He told me Javier has helped him numerous times with hiring escorts when he travels, and he was a great contact to have in New York City. I told him I would love to talk to him and see if he has any work for me while I am in the city the following week, and he agreed to call Javier and give him my contact info.

I got cleaned up, dressed and began packing up my clothes. The room was a mess with T-shirts, jeans, and ball caps lying everywhere, but I somehow managed to find everything I came in with. After I gave Jimmy an awkward hug, he slipped me seven hundred dollars and thanked me for taking the time to see him. I left the meeting feeling worn out and headed home to take a nap before the Halloween weekend festivities began.

Chapter Nine

One Week in New York

Part One

I went to New York City, and this is what basically happened during my seven-day visit. I got hired as a stripper; I stole an iPad from my first customer; I almost got arrested; a cab driver showed me his dick; I got kicked out of the apartment where I was staying; I saw a man get peed on in a urinal by numerous patrons of a bar; I saw nude go-go boys get blown by nearly everyone in the bar (sleazy sex is still alive and well in NYC); I woke up to news that a local bartender in Vegas was shot in the back, neck, and head thirty times by a jilted lover; and I saw a psychic who told me I had been an unwanted pregnancy.

I got to New York on a Tuesday. Three months before I arrived, I had asked my friend Joe if I could stay with him and his roommates in Astoria, and he said of course. I asked numerous times if had cleared it with his two roommates, and each time he said he had. One week was a long time to stay with someone, especially in a city like New York, where people are already basically living on top of each other.

After I got to New York, I took a cab to his place and saw that his room was a complete disaster. Apparently, I was later told by his friends and roommates, he had spent hours cleaning for me, and yet there was dirty and clean laundry everywhere, all sorts of shit pouring out of his closet and from underneath his bed, and the items on the bookshelf were covered in a thick layer of dust. It looked as if there were clothes in between the wall and the bed and he was sleeping on T-shirts, socks, and pajama pants. I had no clue where I was supposed to sleep and was confused as to what his definition of "cleaning" was.

Okay, Christopher... calm down and breathe. He very graciously offered me his place and you are trying to save money, not spend money while you are here. Suck it up, deal with it, and be grateful. I told myself and I did. I am a bit of a snob when it comes to being neat and organized, and I knew Joe and his roommates had graciously opened their home to me, so I had to just get over whatever it was I feeling and make the best of the situation.

Later that night Joe and I decided to go to the gym and work out. Afterward we walked home and grabbed a bite to eat at a falafel place down the street from his apartment. The food was decent and cheap, and it was nice to catch up with Joe after not seeing each other for five months. During our meal, I received a phone call from a client asking if I was free that night, and I said sure. I hated doing last-minute appointments, but sometimes you had to take what you get, and not every client was going to book something with you weeks in advance. Joe and I finished our food and went back to his place, where I showered, douched, and got ready. It was getting pretty late, and I wasn't at all familiar with the New York City subway system, so I decided to call a car service. The car came within ten minutes and I hopped in and was on my way to the Upper East Side.

As we drove into Manhattan I felt like everything on the route we were taking looked vaguely familiar. I had been to New York the year before and I wasn't sure if I had been to this area then or if it just looked familiar. I had no sense of direction in this city, so I just figured it looked similar to somewhere I had been before or had seen on *Sex and the City*. The car stopped in front of a building that looked even more familiar. I approached the doorman and he greeted me and let me in. I went to the man at the front desk to give him my name, so he could call up to the client's apartment. Again, even the doorman and front desk attendant looked and sounded familiar. *Have I been here before?* As I went up in the elevator, I realized I had to have been here before, but I couldn't figure out who I was about to see or if it was the same apartment number as last time. I got off on the thirty-second floor and walked down the long hallway toward the end of the hall. I knocked on the door and a man who looked completely coked out answered. He was twitching, anxious, sweaty, and clearly fucked up. Immediately I knew exactly where I was and remembered I had seen him the year before. The man lived in one of the penthouses in the building, but it surprisingly looked like a shitty apartment. It hadn't been decorated since the 1990s and looked pretty drab and depressing. The place was fairly clean, but it all seemed so dated and not what you would expect from a New York City penthouse. The furniture was old and the "white" sofa was stained. I said hi and asked if he remembered me. He looked me up and down a few times but had no idea who I was.

"I was here a year ago. We met last fall," I said, expecting to see a look of familiarity in his eyes, but he was clueless.

"Really?" he asked, still clearly confused and clearly fucked up. He didn't remember who I was, but I guess it really didn't matter. I remembered the guy was nice enough, but just like last year, he was sweaty, sniffling, and shaky. He wasn't bad-looking, but his fucked -up demeanor left me feeling a little on edge. I was never sure if clients who were cracked out, partying, or stoned were going to flip out on me, pass out, or have a heart attack. I had visions of being the naked hooker with a sheet draped around my body as the paramedics arrived after his heart stopped beating. I imagined they would start asking me who I was and would have to inevitably say I am an escort, and they would look at me with disgust and disdain and think I was the one who gave him the drugs and killed him with my out-of-this-world sexual techniques. This was all highly unlikely, but it's what my imagination would create as I sat there with a cracked-out client. I generally attract a "vanilla" type of clientele, but every so often I would get someone who was on something, and I would spend the entire time during our session on edge and unsure of whether or not they would trip out.

He asked me if I minded him doing a few lines of coke and offered me some too. I politely declined and told him to go ahead and do whatever he wanted. I didn't mind if the client was doing coke or smoked a joint, but I would usually draw the line at meth and crack and ask they didn't smoke it in front of me. He went to the kitchen table and snorted a few lines and took a moment to let it work. He started taking off his clothes, so I did the same and folded them neatly on the stained sofa that was directly underneath a large mirror hanging on the wall. He walked over to me wearing only a Star of David necklace and saggy black dress socks. He turned me around and pressed his body against my backside and started moaning like he was in pure ecstasy. I didn't really do anything, but I don't think he cared. He was just grinding his soft, shriveled-up coke dick on my ass cheeks and moaned like he was experiencing the best feeling ever.

Suddenly he stopped and asked, "Hey, do you know Adam Killian?"

Adam was a very well known porn star I had worked with in the past, so I said "Yes, I do".

"Wow... that's so cool. He's so hot. He's going to be in New York next week, and I'm going to hire him. I really wish he was here with us right now."

I wasn't sure how to take this, so I just said "Yeah, he's really hot. That could be a lot of fun."

"Oh my God, that would be so hot," he replied as he grinded his hips into me harder and harder.

"Look in the mirror," he told me, and I did so.

I smiled and said, "That's really fucking hot," and I made eye contact with him as he grinded himself deeper into my ass cheeks.

"Oh my God, that's so hot. Okay... let's go to my room," he directed me, and I followed him to the next room. He lay on the bed and asked me to straddle his legs but face away from him. I did as I was told and sat directly beneath his balls and popped my ass out. He just felt it lightly and jerked himself off and kept saying, "Oh my God," over and over again. I just sat there wondering if I should be doing anything or saying anything to make this more enjoyable for him, but it felt like I was doing enough and he was perfectly happy just jerking his dick and lightly touching the soft blond hairs on my ass.

"Yeah, that's it. Pop that ass out," he said, and I popped it out even more.

A minute or two went by and there was silence. Finally I said, "Are you ok?"

"Yeah, totally... thanks," he responded. "That was hot."

"Did you cum already?" I asked.

"Oh yeah, a few minutes ago. Thanks, that was just what I needed."

I felt a little silly sitting there popping my ass out not knowing what was going on behind me, but I guess he was satisfied, so I climbed off and headed to the bathroom to grab him a towel. After he cleaned the cum off his belly, he got up and handed me a clean towel from the bathroom and I jumped in the shower to rinse off. When I got out of the bathroom there was no small-talk so we just said our good-byes, I collected my money, and was on my way. I looked at my watch and saw that I was in his place for no more than twenty minutes.

Wow... that was easy money, I thought. I was still surprised he had no clue who I was, but I guessed he must hire guys a lot and he probably gets them confused or forgets who they are. Either way, I was fine with it. I said good night to the doorman on my way out and caught a cab to head back to Astoria.

It had been a long day of traveling and I was happy to crawl into bed with Joe, even though the sheets were dirty and there were piles of dirty and clean clothes surrounding us. Joe and I were both about six-feet-tall grown men in a twin bed, but I didn't care. It was cramped and a little uncomfortable, but we snuggled up close to each other, and I passed out.

The following day I went to the gym with Joe again, did a few errands around Astoria with him, and packed my stuff up to head to Manhattan for the night. I had a seven o'clock appointment with a man named Joshua in Midtown before heading to a club to dance that night. I arrived at Joshua's around seven and he greeted me with a handshake at the door. He was incredibly handsome yet very short (at least compared to me). He must have been no more than five foot five, and I felt like I was towering over him.

"Damn... you really are a big boy, aren't you" he laughed.

I smiled and said, "I guess so."

He invited me in, and we took a seat on a large sectional sofa in his massive two-bedroom penthouse overlooking the city. His place was quite the opposite of Joe's place in Astoria and the shit-box penthouse I was in the night before. He sipped something that looked like a scotch on the rocks and told me about himself. He was in his forties, good-looking, a lawyer, and probably had more money than I will ever see. It was odd to think this man was paying me for sex when I would have gladly let him fuck me for free. New York City was odd in that a majority of the men who called me were incredibly good-looking and rich. Sometimes they were much younger than the men I usually saw, who were generally in their fifties, sixties, and seventies. This left me questioning why this was the case here in New York City but not in Las Vegas. Why couldn't I find a husband like these clients back home?

Was this the universe's way of telling me to move to New York City, or were these men still single for a reason? Who knows...? I was scheduled to be there with him for an hour and it was nice to enjoy myself with someone I might have even possibly paid to sleep with. He wanted me to stay longer than an hour, but I told him I had a dancing gig at eight-thirty that evening. He said okay and thought it would be best if we got started.

He walked over to one of the counters in the kitchen and took out a small bag of cocaine. *Again?* I thought. Were all New York gay men huge coke heads? He asked if I minded or if I wanted any, but again I politely declined.

After he snorted a few lines, he walked over to me and grabbed my hips and brought me in close for a kiss. We started to make out and I had to hunch over to reach his lips. I was wearing my large black combat boots, which added another two inches to my six-foot-one frame, so I had to accommodate his size by leaning over to make this work. We made out and it felt great. I could taste the cocaine in his saliva, and it was weird to be tasting it when you were not actually snorting lines yourself. He started removing my clothes and I assisted him by undoing the straps on my boots and my belt. He caressed my chest and started licking my nipples, which were at a perfect for height, considering my nipples were just below his eye level. I removed his shirt and pressed his chest in closer to me. He was warm, and I could feel his heart beating through his chest. It was going pretty fast and I wasn't sure if it was because of the excitement of the sexual experience, the cocaine, or both.

He pulled down my pants and started rubbing my dick through my underwear. My dick was already hard and the head was poking out the top of my Calvin Klein briefs. He finally grabbed my dick and started stroking it and then bent over to suck it. His mouth was small, so it kind of hurt as I felt the head of my dick being scraped by his teeth. I tried to bear it for as long as possible until I pulled him up to kiss him and move on to something else.

I fully stepped out of my boots, jeans, and underwear and turned around to press my ass against his dick. He grinded his dick around my ass and I spread my cheeks apart farther to invite him to keep going and get ready to fuck me. He spit on his cock to lube it up to fuck me and kept getting the head closer into my hole. I wanted to tease him with my ass, so I let him keep going until he put the head of his dick in my hole. He let out a loud sigh and said, "That feels amazing". I let him keep going for a few seconds until I pulled his dick out and turned around to kiss him. I went to go find my bag with all my supplies. He walked to the kitchen and snorted another few lines off the marble countertop. I returned to the window where we had been before and opened the condom. I handed it to him, poured some lube on my fingertips, and lathered up my hole for him to fuck me. I turned my back to him and placed my hands on the padded bench in front of the window that overlooked the city. I popped my ass out and bent my legs to make it easier for him to enter my hole, and he slid his dick in. His dick wasn't huge but it felt good, and he seemed to like it. He started fucking me and it felt nice. Not only that but I had one of the best views in Manhattan overlooking the city. It had started to rain a little bit outside and I watched as it hit the window and listened as the wind started to blow. The city looked so nice in front of me I nearly forgot what was happening behind me.

We decided to move it into the bedroom and made our way down the hall. His place was huge, and the bedrooms were massive compared to others I'd seen in New York City. I didn't even want to know how much he spent on this place because I'm sure it was much more than the cost of my house, yet my place was about three times the size. The master bedroom was beautifully decorated, and he had a large queen-sized bed covered in pillows. It looked like a showroom bed you'd see in a furniture store, and it matched everything else in the room.

We climbed on his bed and began making out like crazy and pressing ourselves into each other's bodies harder and harder. He asked me to turn onto my stomach and strapped on another condom and began fucking me again for a few minutes until his phone rang. He pulled out, looked at the number, and said, "Shit... I have to take this one. I'm sorry," and walked out of the room.

I lay on the bed and closed my eyes. He had the air going and it started to feel chilly in the room. I cuddled up in the fetal position thinking he was going to come back in, but he didn't. I looked at the clock on the DVR and saw we had only twenty minutes until I had to get going. I rested my eyes and fell asleep for about another ten minutes until I jolted out of bed, worried I had overslept and was going to be late. I climbed out of the bed and walked down the hall and saw Joshua talking on the phone dealing with some kind of business.

"Is everything okay?" I asked softly, and he gave me a thumbs-up and smiled and continued talking to whomever was on the other end of the line.

He suddenly stopped the conversation and said, "Hey, can you hold on one second?" to the person on the other end of the phone and turned to me and said, "You know what... I'm going to be on the phone for a few minutes, so feel free to shower or whatever. I have to deal with some work stuff." I nodded and smiled. "There's a clean towel for you in the guest bathroom in the hall," he said.

I told him, "Thanks," and made my way down the hall to shower. We hadn't really done much of anything, but I figured I might as well shower and smell fresh before I head to a club and get all sweaty again. When I came out from the bathroom he was off the phone and apologized for having to deal with other things. I said it was fine and he said he really wanted to see me again while I was in New York. I told him I was definitely interested and he should call or text me the following day to set something up. He handed me the money and gave me an extra hundred, which I thought was incredibly generous, considering we hardly did anything and the meeting felt better than most hook-ups I had had in the past few months. I bent over to hug the little guy and was on my way to the club to dance that night.

The week before I had come to NYC, Jimmy, my client who asked me to continuously change shirts, walk around the room, and massage his shoulders, got me connected with Javier, the guy that hosts special events in clubs in New York City with male dancers. Javier and I talked on the phone and he told me I could work for him and make some money dancing at a club event he was hosting while I was in town. Javier was a nice guy from the beginning, though I was a little apprehensive about working at the event—it did sound seedy. When we met, I was surprised to see that Javier was not only incredibly nice and a professional businessman, but also absolutely gorgeous.

I arrived at the club around 8:05 p.m. and it was dead. There were already ten to fifteen dancers and ten to fifteen bar patrons. I was confused... one man to one dancer... how was anyone going to make money dancing for tips? I put on my best pair of slutty stripper underwear and began to circulate the club. Although I met some nice guys, nobody was spending money. Time went on and the alcohol was flowing, and guys were slowly starting to tip and go into the backroom with their favorite dancers.

It had been two hours and I still hadn't made any money. Instead, I felt like Julie from the *Loveboat* walking around asking:

"Are you having fun?"

"Where are you from?"

"Did you come here alone?"

"Oh, wow... it's your birthday?"

"So your wife is out of town?"

"Oh, really? You've never done this before?"

And so on...

Finally, a man with a giant duffel bag walked up to me, set his stuff down at my feet, and asked for a drink at the bar. He looked at me and I smiled and jokingly asked, "Do you always carry luggage with you when you go to clubs?"

"I just got back from a trip and I came here." He seemed drunk and was staggering a little bit as he stood at the bar to order a drink.

"I see. What's in the bag?"

"The usual... clothes, shoes, condoms, leather hood, rope, poppers, handcuffs, harness, ball gag, and some other leather gear." He smiled, although his eyes looked bloodshot and were half closed.

"Really? Wow. So you carry that stuff around with you all the time?"

"I'm just fucking with you," he slurred and smiled. He seemed a little sloppy, even though it was only about 10 p.m. He looked at me and said, "Listen, I know what you're selling, and I know I'm not going to get anything from you 'cuz you're straight, so fuck off."

Should I have been offended he thought I was straight, or excited to know I could actually pull off butch as I stood there in my skimpiest underwear?

"Actually, I'm not straight. I'm gay."

"Yeah, right. None of the dancers here are gay. Listen, I've done this before and I know exactly what's going to go down so don't bother, kid." Apparently, most of the male dancers were straight at these events and I guess this man had not gotten what he wanted in the past.

I assured him I was very, very, very gay and asked him if we wanted to go to the backroom. He looked me up and down and asked what he would get. I explained how it all worked and I would do a lap dance for him for twenty dollars per song. He said it was fine, but he had a special request. When I asked what it was, he told me he wanted me to rape him. I couldn't tell if he was kidding or not, but I was speechless.

"Sir... it's not that kind of club," I said when I finally found my voice. "And we're not allowed to rape people here. Sorry."

"Well, that's what I want, so unless you're going to rape me with no safe word, then I'm not interested."

Holy shit, I thought, *New Yorkers are full out with their sex.*

"Sir, I can bring you back there, and I can get rough with you, but I can't really rape you. Those are the rules."

"Okay, fine, whatever. That works."

I grabbed him by his collar and yanked him closer to me. I demanded he pick up his bag and come with me, which he seemed to be into, and then I dragged him to the backroom. I told him to set his stuff down and take off his suit jacket. He did as he was told, and I grabbed him by his shirt and hurled him across the room. The drunken bastard went flying into the wall and fell against a bench and onto the floor. The man looked dead and lifeless lying there.

Oh shit, I thought. *Did I just kill him?*

The man had wanted to get rough, but I think I went too far. I ran over to him and everyone in the backroom stopped to see what was going on. It was kind of a funny sight to see a dark room full of strippers stop giving their lap dances and turn around to see what happened. Everyone seemed concerned and started whispering and asking what the fuck had just happened. A barback came over and asked the man if he was okay, and he said yeah, and we helped him up. Once the barback had gone, the drunken man said to me, "I told you... no safe word." It was clear this man knew exactly what he wanted and I guess I had to play the role of a rapist that night. I couldn't help but think what the fuck was going on and how did this become my life, but I did as I was told.

I danced for six songs and basically spent the time roughing him up, choking him, smacking him around, and he seemed to like it. We didn't do anything too crazy, but he seemed to be enjoying himself, even though he wasn't getting completely physically abused like he had hoped. By the sixth song, the man looked like he was going to either pass out or throw up all over me, so I figured it was time for a break. I climbed off his lap and asked him if he was okay.

"Yeah, I'm fine," he shouted "Let's get another drink."

I took his Black American Express card and went to the bar and ordered us both a drink. It was time to wrap this deal up and get paid for my six songs. He signed out the check, and I told him I had to excuse myself and needed the money for the dances.

"I'm not paying you until you rape me," he said.

"I told you, I can't do that. This isn't that kind of club."

"Well, then, you're not getting your fucking money."

I was in disbelief. "You have to. Its twenty bucks a song, and I gave you six dances." I started to feel like a whiny little kid who was just robbed at his lemonade stand by the neighborhood bully. What did he mean he wasn't going to pay me? I just gave him six lap dances and I figured it was an unwritten rule for strippers that you had to pay them for their services.

"I'm not paying you," he said, throwing his hands up. Then he pushed past me and walked off.

I went to find Javier and explained the situation, and he was even more surprised than I was.

"What the fuck? Are you serious? This has never happened before. Where is he?" asked Javier.

"I don't know... I think he's up front," and Javier was off to look for him.

I had a feeling this guy probably wasn't going to pay me a dime, so I went to the backroom and saw he left his jacket and bag. I picked the bag up, took it downstairs, and hid it. I came back upstairs and asked Javier what was going on, and he said the man wasn't going to pay me. I told Javier if the man didn't pay I was not going to give him his shit back. Javier was doing his best to resolve the situation, and he went to speak to the man again, but he figured this man wasn't going to give in.

I went back downstairs to go through his bag and see if I could at least find a wallet or driver's license to see who this asshole was. I opened the bag to find an iPad, a leather hood, a rope, a harness, two boxes of condoms, handcuffs, gym shoes and shorts, a ballgag, three bottles of poppers, toiletries, and leather gloves. *What the fuck?* This man wasn't lying. He seriously wanted someone to rape him, or at least torture him a bit. I decided the iPad was the only thing of value, so I put it in my bag and went up to see if they got my money from him.

I eventually found Javier, and he told me the man refused to give me any money. "Listen, the guy wants his shit back and he's gonna call the cops if you don't give him his stuff. We seriously can't have the cops here because they'll shut this party down, so I'll give you eighty bucks of my own money if you please just give him back his stuff."

Javier was being so nice and was the perfect mediator. Who would have thought the organizer of male strip events was such a peacemaker? I wanted to hug him. It was nice to see that not everyone in this shady industry was a slime ball. I went to get his bag but kept the iPad, mainly because this guy was an asshole and I kind of wanted to fuck with him. I've never stolen before, and it is definitely not in my character to do so, but I felt a little wrapped up in this stripper drama, and perhaps stealing was the next step in my downward spiral of creating the future Lifetime movie of my life.

I handed the bag over to Javier, and he took it to the entrance of the bar and threw it on the road, and the asshole went scrambling to pick the stuff off the street and collect his shit.

Business picked up that night and I made good money. I ended up meeting a really nice man named Benjamin, who I talked to for about thirty minutes. He wanted to spend some private time with me, but he really wanted to also buy me a lap dance from another dancer. He told me it made him feel really good to see good-looking guys happy, and it would please him if I chose one of the dancers I liked and got a lap dance. I asked if he was serious, and he told me he was. He had been coming to these events since they started and had spent years going to the infamous Gaiety Theatre in Times Square as well as other male strip joints throughout the years. He knew all of the dancers and had been with all of them at one time or another. He asked me who I liked, and immediately I told him I was into the hot, hairy, muscled guy standing across the room. Benjamin told me his name was Teddy, and he was a great guy. He had seen him a few times in the club and a few times outside the club as well. Benjamin asked if he was sure that was the guy I wanted and I said yes.

Suddenly I got really nervous thinking about getting a lap dance from this hot guy standing across from me, and I began to start feeling like a client. Benjamin brought him over to me and my mouth became dry and I was having a hard time getting out the right words. We made small-talk, and Teddy was very nice and extremely sweet. The whole thing began to get weird when I thought how I already had almost $1,200 in my underwear, shoes, and socks from giving guys dances that night, yet here was a dancer in front me who someone else was going to buy for me to spend a few songs with.

Teddy asked if I wanted to go to the backroom, and I said sure. Benjamin went up to Javier and asked him to do us a favor and lower the lights a little bit more so we could have some more privacy. Benjamin gave Javier money to let us use one of the larger areas known as the champagne room, which was sectioned off for VIP patrons. Teddy led me by the hand and through the beads to the vinyl-covered sofa in the back. He brought me in close to him and I nearly melted as our bodies touched.

What was happening? Guys would sometimes spend hundreds to thousands of dollars to be with me, and this one guy brings me in for a hug and I nearly melted into the floor. How did I become the client? He told me to take a seat and he began to perform for me. He had absolutely no rhythm and he looked completely ridiculous dancing to the music being played. I didn't care though... he looked like the man of all my fantasies and I just enjoyed watching him. He climbed on top of me and straddled his giant hairy tree-trunk legs around me and started grinding my dick with his ass, and flexed his muscles for me. The whole thing seemed ridiculous and I wanted to tell Teddy he didn't need to work so hard. I wanted to tell him I don't usually have to pay for it, so there was no need to put on a show for me. All I wanted to do was hold him close, smell him, and feel his body next to mine. I didn't need the badly choreographed dance moves, the flexing, or him saying, "Oh yeah... you like that baby?"

Teddy told me he was a hundred percent completely straight, so he probably wouldn't get hard, but I didn't care. He seemed perfectly okay with doing what he was doing, and I just enjoyed feeling him on top of me. Between having sex with my client earlier and giving about thirty lap dances, I was exhausted and didn't even care. I wasn't in the mood to get off, and my time with Teddy wasn't even about fucking, jerking off, or having an orgasm. He continued dancing on top of me and I leaned in to hug his massive body. I wasn't interested in his dick or how hard it could get. I just wanted to feel his body next to mine and it felt amazing, A rush came over me. I had sex and body contact with people every day, but this felt different and it left me speechless. I didn't want it to end, but knew that after about six songs, it was time to pack it up. I began to ask where Benjamin was, and Teddy said he was waiting for us outside the room.

"Didn't Benjamin want to watch us do stuff?" I asked. I figured he would at least want some kind of show if he was paying to give another dancer a lap dance.

"Nah. Benjamin just wanted you to have fun."

"Oh, wow. Okay," I said in disbelief. It struck me as odd that this man seriously wanted nothing out of this except for me to have a good time. Teddy and I finished up and we went looking for Benjamin. When we found him outside the room, he asked if I had fun. I smiled, turned red and said, "Yeah. A lot of fun. Thank you." Benjamin was happy to do it, and it made up for the experience earlier that night where I lost out on the money the one guy owed me.

"Hey, listen, Christopher. I was wondering if you would be into going back to Teddy's place with us. He said he's into the three of us getting together." I wasn't sure if I had anything left in me to give anyone, but the idea of getting to experience more of Teddy was tempting. At this point, I was so exhausted from the day walking around the city, meeting my client, dancing in the club for five hours, all the lap dances and standing on my feet, I wasn't sure if I would be able to make it through anymore.

"Teddy lives close to here, and if we go back to his place, you guys can do whatever you want and I'll watch. All I need to do is stop by the bank first. Your rate is three hundred dollars, right?"

"Yes, three hundred," I said. So Benjamin was going to pay me to watch me get together with a man hotter than the ones I even fantasized about? How could I say no to that? I packed up my stuff, and we were off to find a Chase ATM. Teddy lived close by in a high-rise apartment building in Hell's Kitchen. He lived alone in his one-bedroom, and the place was pretty nice. We sat around talking for a bit, but Benjamin could see I was growing more and more tired as the time approached 3 a.m. We moved into the bedroom to get things started, and Teddy and I began to get undressed. I saw a machine sitting next to his bed with a hose coming out of it attached to a face mask similar to something you'd see in an operating room.

"Is that for snoring?" I ask.

"Yeah. I had to get it because my snoring drives my girlfriend crazy. I am the loudest sleeper and she can't stand it when she spends the night."

Does your girlfriend know you're bringing guys back to the room? I wanted to know, but instead I just smiled and nodded. A snoring machine and a girlfriend? Definitely not two things I want to associate with the man of my dreams before we were about to get it on. I had to block these images out as we started to fool around.

Teddy wasn't hard, but he turned on his Oscar-winning acting skills and really pretended to get into it with me. We went at it for a few minutes, and I began stroking my cock. I knew I could cum anytime, but I wanted to make it last for at least a few minutes. Benjamin continued to watch us and stroke his dick as Teddy started fucking my mouth with his cock, growing harder and harder. His dick went from limp, to semi-hard, and I guess whatever it was he was fantasizing about began to work, because he seemed to eventually get into it. I kept stroking my dick, and Teddy began thrusting his cock down my throat deeper and deeper. Finally, I came and Benjamin rushed down to lick up every last drop of my load, and soon after he also came. Teddy lay next to me and let me suck his dick until he came, and we all lay there for a few minutes before we got up and collected our stuff. It was already well after three, and Benjamin offered to drive me back to my place. He lived close to where I was staying, so he didn't mind dropping me off on his way home. We said our good-byes to Teddy and made our way home. Benjamin and I agreed to stay in touch, and he continues to check in with me every few months or so to see how I am doing.

I crawled into bed that night exhausted and worn out. I was satisfied with how everything turned out and the money I made, but part of me was still pissed off about the guy who ripped me off. I have a hard time letting go of things, so I decided to take out his iPad and see what was on it. His Facebook account was open, so I wrote on his wall, "I just wanted to let everyone know I am a drunk-ass tool," and went to bed. The next day, I woke up to find his wall flooded with messages like, "Yeah... we know," or "I could have told you that twenty years ago." Apparently, everyone already knew this man's character.

Later that night, Javier contacted me and told me he knew I had the iPad and I had to give it back. The guy had returned to the bar with the police, and they were going to arrest me if I didn't give it back to him immediately. Javier reasoned with them and they agreed they wouldn't press charges if I gave the iPad back to him and he would return it to the cops. Okay, this stripper drama was getting to be too much and I knew I had gone too far. I told him I would give it back, mainly because Javier was pretty sweet, and the last thing I wanted to do was give him any trouble after he went out of his way to bring me into his club to dance. We agreed to meet the following night so I could give him the iPad, but before I did, I decided to have another look on it.

This man had posted several ads on various websites and responded to dozens of ads inquiring about anonymous hotel fuck-fests and ads inquiring about torture, rape scenarios, and severe physical abuse and humiliation. This guy was seriously looking into getting tied up, gagged, raped, and humiliated, and he was a frequent user on the Craigslist personals section. I was a little shocked but reminded myself that this stuff must happen all the time, and I guess I shouldn't be surprised, because it was New York City, after all.

Part Two

After discussing with Javier where we were going to meet so I could give him back the iPad, I was sitting in Joe's living room trying to figure out how I was going to get myself into Manhattan that afternoon. Ever since I got to town I had been trying to figure out the subway system and kept resorting to taking cabs and the available car services in Astoria. I knew the trains were cheaper and easy once you got to know them, but after running around all day and dealing with clients, I preferred the car service. Who wouldn't?

That afternoon Joe was at work and I was in the apartment, and one of his roommates named Scott was getting ready to head out for the day. Earlier, I had received a text from Joe saying his roommates were upset with him and they wanted me out of their apartment. I had asked him why and he told me he had no idea. I decided to confront Scott now, but told myself to remain calm because I was the guest in their home and I was sure it was just a misunderstanding.

Scott told me—and the other roommate later confirmed it—that Joe had never asked them if I could stay with them; instead, they were told the day I arrived that I would be staying for two days and I had been given a spare key for the apartment. On day three of my visit, they were confused as to why I was still hanging around the apartment and began to get pissed off. Their anger wasn't directed toward me but at Joe. Apparently, according to his roommates, communication was not something he was good at, and neither was paying bills on time, cleaning, and being courteous. Scott told me I could stay if I wanted to, but he at least wanted to make me aware of the situation.

"No, thanks," I said. "I came here for a vacation not to be in the middle of some roommate drama bullshit." I thanked him for letting me stay with them and apologized for the misunderstanding. I told him I had done everything on my part to be sure it was okay that I stayed there. Joe, on the other hand, had acted oblivious to what was happening, and I was left dealing with the brunt of his housemates' anger and frustration. Even when I tried to ask Joe about the situation via text message, he had no idea what was going on and couldn't understand why his roommates were ganging up on him.

I had no energy to deal with any of this so I just decided to wash my hands of it and get a place to stay in the city. I ended up finding a hotel online, called a car service to pick me up, and made my way into the city within the next hour.

I was upset by the whole situation and annoyed I was now going to have to pay about eight hundred dollars to stay in a hotel for a few nights. I was going to be making money while I was there, but there wasn't much point in spending all this money to go to New York if all the money I was making was going directly to pay for my trip. I was trying to be a cost effective hooker here and barely breaking even was not was I was aiming for. Oh well, I knew I had to change my mindset and try not to focus on my anger or disappointment in the situation because I knew nothing could change it.

On my way into the city to my hotel, a young man in his late twenties named Marcelo began texting me. He made it clear he really wanted to meet up but was unsure as to whether or not it would fit into his schedule that day. I suggested we meet that afternoon because I wanted to have time to go get tickets to a Broadway show that night. We threw some times back and forth and he basically told me it was going to have to be within an hour or so or it probably wouldn't happen because he had to be somewhere later that afternoon. Now that I was paying for the hotel I felt like I was going to have to literally sell my ass even more to make a profit from this trip. I agreed to meet him at four o'clock in my hotel room.

I got to the hotel shortly after three, and I knew I was going to be pressed for time before he got there, so I didn't waste a moment as soon as I checked in and got to my room. The hotel was called the Pod Hotel on East Fifty-first Street, and it looked like it had been renovated recently. The room was definitely "cute," even though there was only a few feet of space around the perimeter of the double bed, and the window faced a large brick building. The room was modern, simple, and looked like it had been furnished by IKEA. I figured it would suffice. I opened my suitcase and began unpacking and throwing shit everywhere as I searched for an enema in my bag. As soon as I found it I began the process of cleaning myself out and making sure I was squeaky clean for Marcelo. As I sat on the toilet, I noticed I could literally touch the shower and bed with both my hands at the same time. Damn... you gotta love New York City hotels.

After I was done, I jumped in the shower and scrubbed every part of my body to make sure I smelled impossibly fresh and ready for my client. It felt like a mad rush to get settled into the room, make it look presentable, and get myself ready before he arrived, but I somehow managed to do it all before he knocked on my door at 4:01.

I opened the door to find one the hottest Italian men I had ever seen. He was about five-foot-ten, with black hair, tanned skin, and a chiseled masculine face. He was standing there with a jacket and backpack on with a nervous smile on his face. He looked like he wanted to hurry up and get in my room in fear of someone he knew seeing him. I smiled and invited him in immediately. I didn't know what this guy wanted to do, but whatever it was I knew I would do it willingly. I thought, *This gorgeous man is going to pay me to have sex with him? I would gladly pay him twice my hourly rate to simply stare at his naked body and maybe touch his chest.* One word to describe him would be breathtaking.

As soon as he stepped inside the room, he asked if he could hang up his jacket. I pointed to the closet, which was directly behind him, and told him to feel free to throw everything in there. He took out a hanger and neatly placed his jacket on it and hung it back up and put his bag in the closet. His biceps were huge and his pecs were busting through his tight gray V-neck T-shirt, which looked like he bought from American Apparel. He was wearing a gold chain around his neck, a gold watch, and a gold ring on his right index finger. Immediately I thought, *What a fucking hot-ass Guido,* and I couldn't believe I was about to have sex with this closeted, hot, overly tanned Italian macho man and get paid three hundred dollars to do so.

There was no room to sit, other than the bed, so I offered him a seat and asked him if he wanted one of the two-dollar bottles of water provided by the hotel on the desk. He politely declined and I smiled and went to sit down with him. We sat there in silence for a few seconds before I tactlessly asked him, "So, you're actually gay?"

He gave a slight smile, laughed a little, and said, "Kind of, yeah. I mean I date girls sometimes but I really hate the whole gay dating scene. But I guess you could say I'm more gay than straight."

"Oh, so you've been with men, then?" I asked.

"Yeah, but it's always kinda weird," he said. "Guys are weird and sometimes it's a pain in the ass trying to date them or hook up."

"Isn't it the same thing with girls, though?"

"Well, yeah, true, I guess. Either way it kind of sucks," he said.

He seemed shy and didn't really make much of an effort to make eye contact. I couldn't get a vibe from this guy and wasn't sure what exactly he wanted. I wasn't even sure if he was into me or not. I knew I wanted to rip his clothes off and let him do every possible, filthy, disgusting thing he had ever fantasized about doing to another man to me, but I tried to remain calm and not too eager. I reminded myself that desperation isn't a good look on anyone.

We sat there for a minutes in silence, and I figured I was going to have to be the one to take action so I eventually leaned in and kissed his neck. He smelled of sweat mixed with a cologne that reminded me of Pino Silvestre. I always enjoyed the smell of a man without the added scent of cologne, but with him I didn't care. I was hoping he was the type of man that got into rimming, because I wanted to spread his legs and eat his ass and get his scent all over my face and be able to smell it the rest of the night as I sat through whatever show I decided to see.

Eventually my kisses along his neck move toward his mouth and he turned to kiss me. He was definitely into it and seemed almost scared to let himself go. I imagined he probably had years of repressed sexual fantasies he wanted to act on, and I wanted to be the guy he acted out every fantasy with. We continued making out and eventually I laid him down on his back. As we kept kissing, I began caressing his chest and couldn't get over how huge and firm his pecs were. *How in the hell was this happening to me and did this man even realize he was fulfilling some of my sexual fantasies being there?* I was a tall skinny kid from Saskatchewan and we never saw men like him where I was from. Even though I had been doing porn for over a year now, I felt like I was about to live out one of my porn fantasies with one of the most gorgeous men I had ever seen.

I began to remove his shirt, and though he still seemed shy, he eventually let me take it off. There was absolutely no way we were going to do this with his shirt on. I wanted to look at his giant pecs as I rode his dick and hold on to them as he tore up my asshole and dropped a load in my ass. I had never let a client fuck me without a condom before, but something came over me as I lay there making out with a man who looked like something out of my dreams. He could shoot a load of cum in my ass, down my throat, on my face... Honestly I didn't care. I lost any ounce of common sense by that point, and he could have told me he had HIV and I probably wouldn't have stopped him from doing whatever he wanted to with me.

I unzipped his pants, pulled down his underwear, and out popped his nine-inch uncut dick. *Are you serious?* This perfect-looking, masculine, muscled Guido also had a perfect cock? I wanted to turn my head toward the ceiling and just start crying out. "thank you. God... thank you. You are so good to me, Jesus..." but I figured it might seem a little dramatic.

As I began to stroke his rock-hard dick, I had to force myself to count to ten before I started going hog-wild sucking it. I slowly kissed down his chest and along his furry little trail of hair on his belly toward his crotch. As I went to put his cock in my mouth, he said, "Whoa, whoa, whoa, whoa, man... You can't do that without a condom."

"What?" I asked.

"I don't do oral without condoms. Sorry."

"I can't even give you a blowjob without a condom?"

"No, man. That's not safe. You mean you give all your clients BJ's without rubbers?"

"Ummm... yeah, pretty much." I said in disbelief that this man was seriously asking such an obvious question.

"Aren't you afraid of diseases and stuff?"

"Well, I get tested every three months, and I am HIV negative. In this line of work you kind of have to take your chances," I said, trying not to sound annoyed. Was this guy seriously trying to lecture me on safe sex? All of a sudden my ultimate sexual fantasy was turning into an after-school special, and I had to fight from rolling my eyes and asking, "Are you serious?" I'm a gay male, I do porn, and I'm an escort. Having oral sex without a condom wasn't exactly risky behavior in comparison to half the shit I knew many other gay men and escorts out there were doing. Maybe I had been sleeping around for too long, maybe I was incredibly jaded, or maybe I had been watching too many Treasure Island Media movies, but I couldn't believe this guy wasn't going to let me suck his dick without a rubber.

"Well, I don't think I'm cool with that, dude. Sorry. Maybe we can just fuck with a condom, then," he suggested. I looked down at his beautiful, picture-perfect cock, and I wanted to roll my eyes and start pouting, but instead I said, "Sure," and reached for the condoms.

He rolled on a Trojan Magnum and squirted a bunch of lube on his dick. I took the bottle of lube and poured out an equal amount onto my hand and lathered it on my hole. I knew I was going to need a lot of grease to get that monster inside me. He slowly eased his cock into me and looked me in the eyes as it went in. It hurt a little at first, but once his giant mushroom head was in it felt amazing. Instantly I could feel it rubbing against my prostate and I gasped. Very few men had been able to make me cum from simply putting their cocks in me, but this felt like it was going to be one of those times. Immediately he started slamming his dick in my ass, and I had to tell him to slow down a few times because he was going to make me cum right away. He obliged and went back to fucking me slowly and kissing me at the same time.

It didn't take long for his slow, long thrusts to turn into long, hard thrusts that made me feel like I was going to cum again. He started going faster and faster and I could see his huge, beefy pec muscles jiggling in front of my face. Goddammit, I wanted his bare cock inside me and I wanted to feel him dump a load inside my ass. How was I stuck with the hottest man I have ever been with and the only thing he'll do (aside from kissing) is fuck me with a rubber? I had lost any ounce of common sense, and I didn't care about the consequences. I just wanted his load in my hole and dripping out my ass.

I looked up at him again and I started to stroke my dick harder and harder. I felt like I was going to cum, but then he stopped, pulled out, grabbed both my thighs, and flipped me around onto my stomach. He shoved his cock back in me and continued pounding away. I screamed as his dick tore up my hole, and he reached around to cover my mouth as he continued fucking me. His giant dick was beginning to hurt, but I didn't care... the pain turned into pleasure and I completely got into this fantasy of him raping my hole and covering my mouth so nobody in the hotel would hear through the paper-thin walls. He kept on fucking me for about two minutes before he pulled out again and flipped me back onto my back.

"I wanna cum like this," he said.

"Ok, sure, yeah... however you want," I agreed.

He shoved his cock back into me one last time. As he went at it again, I worked on my dick in hopes that I would cum at the same time. He thrust his cock in deeper and deeper as he looked down at it going in and out of my hole. Finally he looked at me and said, "Shit, man... I'm gonna cum. You ready for me?"

Of course I was ready. I was ready for it on my face, in my hole, on my chest... wherever. I just wanted him to give it to me! I worked my dick up (even though I had been ready to cum since he initially started fucking my ass) and he drove his dick in deeper and deeper until he finally blew his load.

It took me about five seconds after he came for me to shoot my load all over my chest. He collapsed on top of me, and we lay there for about a minute to catch our breath and regain some energy before getting up. He smiled down at me and I gave him a playful wink and a little kiss. He got up, ripped the condom off, threw it in the garbage, and walked over to the sink to wash his hands. I wasn't sure if this guy was a hypochondriac germaphobe or just petrified of possibly getting something from my hooker asshole, even though he wore a condom. I got him a clean towel and turned the water on so he could take a shower. He hopped in the miniature shower that looked like it was designed for a Barbie doll camper and not a hotel room. It was funny to see such a big burly muscled guy in such a tiny setting.

After he finished cleaning up, he dried off and got dressed, and we made some small-talk. He put his coat back on and grabbed his bag. I'm not sure where this man was headed, but he looked like he was on his way to school. He took a wad of cash out of his inside pocket and handed it to me.

"Here you go, man. Thanks." I leaned in to kiss him and he gave me a little pec on the lips. I guess now that the intensity of the sex was over, he was back to being straight, bi, or whatever. "Take care of yourself, and be careful not to suck too much dirty dick. That shit is dangerous."

Inside my head I was rolling my eyes at his concern, but I smiled and said, "Thanks, man. I'll be good," and saw him out the door. Nice guy, incredibly hot, but wouldn't let me go within an inch of his dick in fear of getting an STD? Wow. That was a first.

It was a little after five p.m. and I wanted to be sure I had enough time to get to the discount TKTS booth in Times Square to find a show to see. When I arrived, I saw that *Follies* with Bernadette Peters was playing, and since I had heard great things about it, I bought a ticket. I somehow managed to get seats in the center of the third row. The show was amazing, and Bernadette Peters and the cast were incredible. I was happy to have had the chance to see it.

After the show, I met up with Javier to give him back the iPad and apologize for everything that happened. He laughed and assured me nothing like that had ever happened at one of his events, and he wanted me to come back and dance for him the next time I was in the city. I agreed, we hugged, and I was on my way.

I decided to go visit the famous gay bar called the Cock. It had quite the reputation for being seedy, skanky, and where pretty much anything goes. I even read a review on Yelp that said someone had defecated on the bar one evening and the entire bar watched. I'm not really into seeing that stuff happen, but it's like a train wreck: how could I not stop by and witness the bawdiness at a club where taking a dump in front of others was not only allowed but encouraged and featured as one of the top reasons to go there?

I hailed a cab and asked the driver if he knew where the Cock was and he said, "Of course, right away, sir," and we took off. I was so impressed and amused that this Indian taxi driver knew where the bar was, but again, I was not surprised. It was New York, after all, and places like the Cock probably have little to no shock value for locals.

As we headed across town, I could see the driver looking at me at the mirror. I asked him how he was and he said, "Very good, very good," with an Indian accent.

"Good to hear. Are you having a good night?"

"Yes, yes, sir. You?"

"Yes, it's good," I replied, smiling at him in the mirror.

He smiled back and asked, "Are you a dancer, sir?"

"Yes, I am. How did you know?"

"You look like one, sir," he said, grinning broadly.

I laughed, "Okay, thanks."

"I like dancers," he told me.

"Oh, really?" I wasn't sure where this conversation was going, but it was amusing and I felt like I needed to see what was going to happen.

"Yes, I do. You're so beautiful, sir." Now I was blushing, completely confused and not sure what to say next. I guess I had always fantasized about fucking a taxi driver, though not a middle-aged, balding cabbie from India.

"You stay in hotel, sir?"

"Yes, I do."

"Where is your hotel?"

"On the West Side on 50th Street," I lied. I was actually staying on the East Side on 51st, but I didn't want this guy showing up to my hotel and waiting for me.

"Oh, nice, nice. Maybe I can pick you up from the bar later and take you back?"

I started laughing nervously and I was unsure if I should tell him to fuck off or just get out and walk. I have to admit, however, that I was a little intrigued by the whole thing, and although he wasn't someone I would peg as my type, I was curious to see how far this man would go.

The ride came to an end, and he said he wanted to show me something. As I leaned forward to pay him, I could see that his dick was out. It was probably eight inches long and raging hard. I burst out laughing and said, "Wow... that's, um... very nice."

"We can't do anything in the cab, but I can come to your hotel later and we can do stuff there." I started to get the church giggles and felt as if I should tip him a bit more, seeing as he was giving me the most interesting ride in a cab I have ever had. I politely declined, gave him a six-dollar tip, and got out to head into the Cock.

As I entered the club, I saw three or four go-go boys dancing on the bar. They weren't exactly beautiful, muscled, or exotic-looking. In fact, they kind of all looked a little torn up, scrawny, and weathered, like they had probably spent a few nights on the streets and had lived a hard life. They—like the club—looked a little haggard and dirty, but maybe this was the look they were all going for? Who knew. As the night wore on, I realized that these go-go boys were not hired on account of their looks but because they were pretty much letting guys do whatever they wanted to them, and they looked like they enjoyed it. As it got later, the dancers began to fondle themselves.

Eventually the underwear came off, and they all revealed their hard-ons. Full frontal nudity? I certainly wasn't opposed. I hadn't seen this since the last time I had gone clubbing in Puerto Rico. Eventually, a lot of the guys in the club began lining up to suck their cocks, and the dancers looked like they loved it. Sometimes, the guys sucking their dick would give them a dollar; other times, they wouldn't and the dancers didn't seem to care either way. The dancers all had erections and were groping each other and fondling themselves as guys continued to line up to suck their dicks. I wasn't disturbed by the fact that these guys were getting sucked off in a sleazy club by dozens of guys; I was more concerned about the guys sucking the dicks. Weren't these men concerned about waking up with a herpes, gonorrhea, or syphilis? A cute lesbian standing nearby leaned over and said to me, "I'm not upset about the cock-sucking going on. I'm more concerned about these men sucking dirty dick. Aren't they worried they're going to catch something like herpes, gonorrhea, or syphilis?"

"OH, MY GOD!" I yelled. "I was thinking the exact same thing!"

We bonded over the show going on in front of us and talked about how sad it was these boys weren't even making decent money to get their dicks sucked by a room of seedy-looking guys. As we were watching the oral sex show, one guy put one of the dancer's dicks in his mouth and went to town on it. There must have been a spilled drink on the floor because after about thirty seconds, he lost his balance and fell on the floor. The cocksuckers lined up behind him hurried to help him up and hoisted him onto a barstool, consoled him, and asked if he was okay. The man who fell put his hand on his forehead, fanning himself, with sheer panic in his eyes. I had just witnessed my first near death cock-sucking experience.

My new lesbian friend looked at me and said, "Oh, my God... did you just see that?" We both burst out laughing.

It was getting late and I wanted to head to one more leather bar before I called it a night, so I said bye to my new lesbian friend and got a cab to take me to one of my favorite bars in New York City, the Eagle.

I entered the building, which was packed on all levels. I got a shot of Jack and a beer at the downstairs bar and walked around. I always loved going to the Eagle when I visited New York and would usually make a few stops there during my stay. Guys were shirtless, in jocks, leather harnesses, making out, their dicks hanging out. It was seedy, and I loved it because it always reminded me of the "dangerous" gay leather bars homophobic televangelists and pastors would tell me as a child I would end up in if I turned out being gay. The Eagle was pure entertainment; it never disappointed me and tonight was no exception. I wandered around and played the part of a voyeur all night and met some very interesting people. Nobody had inhibitions there, especially about talking to others. I liked how guys would just approach me and start talking. Some would walk right up to me and say, "Can I suck your dick?" I would usually always politely decline, but I would thank them for the offer and say, "Good luck tonight," and smile.

After three shots of whiskey and three pints of Stella, I had to go to the bathroom, which at that point had turned into one of the most crowded places in the bar. I saw a man lying in the giant urinal getting pissed on by four or five guys and loving every minute of it. Again, I was astonished to be witnessing something so crazy, yet ultimately not surprised at all because it was New York City after 2 a.m. on a Saturday at the Eagle. After the bathroom show, I washed my hands and got my jacket from the coat check. I headed back to the hotel and got a sandwich at a deli close to where I was staying—a perfect end to an amazing night.

Part Three

On my final day in New York, I woke up to a text from a friend named Brian, a local bartender from Vegas, saying Phil Wells was shot and killed at 5:30 a.m. earlier that day. Phil Wells? I rubbed the sleep out of my eyes and reread the text. I knew the name but couldn't put a face to it. I replied with, "Who's Phil Wells?" and hit send.

I figured we were probably Facebook friends so I logged on and entered his name. His picture came up, and I automatically realized who he was. We weren't close, but he was a bartender at a place called the Garage, and I always saw him when he was working or out with friends at the bars. He was a super nice guy, with the biggest smile on his face at all times. He—along with the other bartenders—was the reason everyone went to the Garage; they were incredibly sweet and polite to everyone. As soon as I saw his picture, I began to read my newsfeed and saw dozens of updates from my Vegas friends about the shooting. Everyone was in shock, crying, panicking, and exchanging information.

I didn't know what was going on, but I tried my best to follow the story all day and read the posts updated every few minutes. It didn't take long for the Las Vegas Metro Police Department to catch the guy who shot him. It was a jilted ex-boyfriend turned stalker who flew to Vegas, checked into a Motel 6, went to the Garage around 5:30 a.m., and fired thirty shots in Phil's back, neck, and head. They caught him before he was boarding a plane back home to Tennessee. I was in disbelief as I read all the posts and watched the local news online. How was this happening? This was something I had only heard about or seen on TV and here it was, unfolding in front of everyone. What dumbfounded me—and upset many others too—was that Phil Wells was a guy who was so incredibly sweet to everyone. Why would someone fly across the country and fire thirty shots into him? It made no sense to me, and my heart ached for Phil's family and for everyone who had lost a friend.

I spent my last day in New York wandering the streets and drinking coffee, still a stunned by the news. The weather was gray, which suited my mood, and my brain felt numb trying to make sense of what had happened.

As I was trying to process everything and make sense of it all, I walked by a psychic shop that I had passed numerous times since I checked in to my hotel. I was curious about it but had been hesitant about going in. I generally only liked to go to psychics and get my cards read when it was someone recommended to me. But I saw that it was only forty dollars for a thirty-minute reading, so I decided to give it a try. I walked in and entered into what appeared to be someone's living room with two men and an older, larger woman. The men were watching TV and the woman was talking very loudly on the phone. They all stopped to stare at me, and I immediately felt awkward, as if I had walked into someone's private home. I wanted to turn around and walk out, but I decided to at least ask about the services they offered.

The younger man led me into the small entryway and told me to have a seat. The room was incredibly tiny and could barely hold a small end table and two chairs. He told me about the services they offered, and I said I would like my cards read. He instructed me to shuffle the deck and cut the cards. After I did so, he began to lay them out in front of me. He took a few minutes to study the cards and he finally looked at me and said, "I'm getting some really strong stuff from you, and I don't think I can read your cards. I'm going to get my mother. She knows all."

This whole situation was a little strange, but I said, "Okay."

Within a few minutes the large woman came out into the sitting room. She introduced herself, and I told her my name and immediately she started coughing. She sounded like she smoked at least a pack of cigarettes a day. After she got over her coughing fit, she sat down. She was missing several teeth, had more facial hair than I had ever seen on a woman, and rather than breathe, she wheezed the entire time I was there. Her appearance was a little startling, but I felt if you wanted to have an interesting experience with a psychic, she was probably the best woman for the job.

As she shuffled the cards, she asked me some basic questions, like where I was from, my age, my zodiac sign, and where I was born. She then instructed me to cut the cards and began to lay them out in front of me. She asked me what my name was again.

"Christopher," I answered.

"Christopher, you were supposed to have some spiritual work done... what happened?" she asked.

I thought about it and realized she was right. "I had met with a psychic three times, but after she forgot about our meeting on two separate occasions, I finally gave up and stopped seeing her."

"I see..." she said. "I see you are in holistic medicine. I see that you have a very long life ahead of you, and you are in great health. I see that you are supposed to be involved in physical fitness somehow, and you are supposed to be a writer... I see you giving seminars. What do you do for work now?"

I hesitated but said, "I do porn. Escort... and dance."

"And do you love this?"

"I love aspects of it, but I'm not sure how long I want to be doing this."

"Do you want to be an actor?"

"I don't think so."

"I don't see any of this in your cards. Acting is not for you. I see you as a writer because you have a gift and you need to pursue that. Unfortunately, though, you have a lot of enemies. People are jealous of you and do not like you. They may seem nice to your face, but behind your back, they are jealous and speak ill of you."

My eyes widened. *Really? People don't like me?* I always tried to be likeable, but I guess everyone has enemies. She told me she definitely sees writing in my future as well as a big move. She told me my aura is that of a sixty-year-old man and I have a lot of negative forces keeping me down. She also told me the love of my life was a dark, handsome, and very jealous man. She sensed a strong P name and asked if I knew anyone with a name that began with P. When I told her I didn't, she kept saying, "P...P... all I see is a P." It was weird because I honestly couldn't think of anyone in my day-to-day life with a P name, so maybe I have yet to find him.

She asked what birth order I was in my family, and I told her I was the youngest. She said I had been an unwanted pregnancy, and at first my father didn't want me. This surprised me, and I was a little shocked. I didn't see that one coming. She said I was looked at as one more mouth to feed. I'm not sure how I felt about that because I never sensed it from my parents growing up. She said it was something I sensed early on in the womb.

Although I was a little bit confused and surprised, I took it all with a grain of salt. The encounter was informative, and I was sure to record the whole session so I could see if her predictions would come to pass in the future. She wanted me to stay and pay an additional two hundred dollars to get some more cleansing done, but I had to politely decline and get on a shuttle bus to LaGuardia. I got up, thanked her, and left to catch my ride to the airport. The information she shared with me wasn't life-changing, but it gave me a lot to think about on the flight home to Vegas.

I didn't realize my week in New York was so eventful until I sat down to write about it. I'm not sure if I'll ever live in New York City, but whenever I go, it never disappoints me and I can't wait to go back.

Chapter Ten

Five Porn Shoots, Three Clients, Painted, and Food Poisoning.

Three weeks after I got back from New York City, I made my way to the West Coast for ten days of shooting porn and a dancing gig at the famous Nob Hill Theatre in San Francisco. I started off my trip in LA for three days, where I shot a scene for men.com with the porn star Phenix Saint.

I had worked for men.com one other time before that, and it was a good experience. The director I worked with was a woman named Laura, and I had had a good time working with her and the rest of her crew. I thought Phenix was decent-looking, but it didn't take me long to realize he was not gay and he was probably just doing porn for the money and/or "fame." The shoot went reasonably well, but I generally found it annoying shooting a scene with a straight man because they had many limitations on what they would and wouldn't do and they always had to have straight porn playing in the background. I understand we all have our things that get us off, but it never helped me reach an orgasm on set or maintain an erections when I had to hear a woman screaming as she's getting fucked in the background. Phenix seemed to really get off on watching girls deep throat large dicks and massive dildos. In one of the scenes he was getting off to, I watched in horror as this pretty, innocent-looking girl gagged on an eleven-inch dildo and giggled after she took it out of her mouth. He seemed to love this and it eventually did the trick and helped him shoot his load all over me.

After the shoot and a few days in LA, I flew to San Francisco for seven days, where I had four shoots lined up and to dance at the Nob Hill Theatre. I had planned the trip to SF months before when Michael Brandon from Nob Hill asked me to come out and be one of their featured performers on a Friday and Saturday night. Around that time I was booked to dance, the casting director and friend Race Cooper also asked me to do a live webcam show for Raging Stallion Studios with

115

two of my favorite directors, Bruno Bond and Steve Cruz. Initially I thought the trip would only be a few days of work and a few days of shooting, but once the porn studios Titan and Hot House heard I was in town, they asked me to be a part of their shoots as well.

All of a sudden my relaxing vacation in San Francisco turned into four porn shoots (three of them back to back) and four shows dancing at Nob Hill. When I tried to spread the shoots out over the seven days I would be in town, I knew it wouldn't be possible to change the dates. My worst fear in shooting all the scenes was that I would be exhausted, worn out, completely drained of cum, and looking horrible on camera. Masturbating four days in a row is one thing, but shooting a quality scene with some of the biggest studios in the industry required rest and being mentally and physically prepared. I hated shooting more than two days in a row because I never felt like my performance was any good and the audience would be able to tell. Sure, we were only filming porn and this wasn't a Broadway production, but I still thought of it as a "performance" and didn't want my name attached to it if it wasn't any good. Everyone in the industry knew that certain bloggers who reviewed gay porn could be complete bitches when reviewing the latest scenes, and the commentators and readers of these blogs were oftentimes worse than the person writing the reviews. When I first started shooting porn this always caused me a little stress when a scene came out, but now I was used to it and rarely read the reviews or comments.

With my schedule now completely booked, I knew I had to be rested and ready to go the minute I landed in San Francisco.

My performance at Nob Hill on Friday night went well, and I had a great time. The audience wasn't too big, but I think it was to be expected, considering it was December and most people were probably at Christmas parties for work or with their families rather than at an all-nude male strip club on a Friday night.

The following day I was scheduled to shoot for Hot House Studios with Marc Dylan. Marc was one of the biggest names in the industry at the time, and he was a good guy to work with. I had met him the previous summer while on a location shoot for Falcon Studios. We were both somewhat new to the industry and had gotten into it around the same time. There was a good group of guys on this shoot, and we all got to know each other a little bit during the three days we spent in Sonoma County. I had been shooting a scene with Trent Locke for a movie called *Right Here, Right Now,* and I felt as if the whole thing was a disaster... I had had an ingrown hair on my chin that had become infected the night before the shoot. Convinced it looked like some kind of STD, I had been paranoid the entire time we were shooting the scene.

Trent, on the other hand, had seemed like he was clearly fucked up on something, and I wasn't sure if he had smoked weed or crack before the shoot or if that was just his personality. The shoot had lasted almost six hours, and near the end I couldn't get hard and cum so I ran inside to grab my bag from the bathroom to dig out a Viagra and chew it up to make it work faster. Somebody was in the bathroom where my stuff was, and I had no time to wait. I started knocking frantically, and finally Marc opened the door.

"Hey," I said. "I'm really sorry, but I need to grab something out of my bag."

"Oh, sure, go for it," he said.

As I frantically began looking for one more magic blue pill in my bag on the ground, I noticed Marc was trying to adjust his dick in his jeans. I could tell he was hard, and I asked him if everything was all right.

"Yeah, sure, man. I just finished my photo shoot, and my dick is so hard... I took a Viagra before we started, and now my dick won't go down." He laughed softly.

All of a sudden I forgot we were on an all-day porn shoot, and I forgot about my limp dick. I didn't care that I was tired, and I wasn't even mad that my scene partner was a complete mess outside. I felt like Marc and I were in some seedy porn video, and the scenario got me hard immediately.

I was on my knees looking for a pill and finally found one. I popped it into my mouth, chewed it up, and swallowed it. I took a sip of water to wash down the bitter taste and continued to watch Marc lightly rub his cock in his jeans. I looked up at him and said something I and many other models had said in countless porn scenes: "Want me to help you take care of that?"

He smiled and said, "Sure man," and then unzipped his jeans. His rock-hard cock fell out and I crawled over to where he was standing and swallowed his dick until it hit the back of my throat. I could already taste his precum, and my dick got even harder. I had to force myself not to touch my dick because I needed to save my cum shot for the camera. Not touching myself was probably one of the most difficult things I had ever done. I have absolutely no self-control when it comes to sucking dick or eating a man's load. Marc started thrusting his dick down my throat, and when he started moaning, I could tell he was already close to cumming.

"Fuck, yeah. That feels good... keep going man." And I did.

He pulled his dick out of my mouth after about a minute and began stroking it. He positioned his cock away from my face and whispered, "I'm gonna cum... fuck I'm gonna cum."

I grabbed his hips. "Shoot your fucking load in my mouth, man... come on. I fucking want it," I begged.

He kept stroking his cock until finally he grabbed my head and blew his load down my throat. He grunted as he drained every last drop, and I swallowed the entire thing.

Immediately I stood up, smiled, and said, "That's exactly what I needed," and ran out of the bathroom to finish my scene with Trent. I came within about two minutes of the final take. All I had needed was the salty aftertaste of Marc's load in my mouth to finally get off.

Marc and I were both known as power bottoms in the industry, so when Hot House told me I was going to be fucking him, I began to get worried. I had been a top before in the past, but it usually required the help of various erectile dysfunction medications like Cialis, Viagra, Trimex, or Caverject. I didn't like using Trimex or Caverject injections to get hard, but sometimes there was no other option if you couldn't get an erection. I enjoyed being a top in my personal life, but I didn't like it when shooting scenes. Being a top required a few things, and the biggest and most important one was a rock-hard erection. For me to maintain an erection, I had to have great chemistry with my scene partner, and I needed the studios who were filming the scene to let me fuck the way I wanted to fuck. If there was no connection between my scene partner and me or if the studio had a us doing a variety of positions that simply did not feel good, then it didn't matter how much Viagra or Caverject I had in me... I simply wasn't going to get hard. Case closed. Oftentimes the sexual positions that felt best between you and your scene partner were not always the best positions to film porn, but like many things in this industry it was just a part of the job.

Marc and I were scheduled to shoot early Saturday afternoon, but our call time kept getting pushed back because the scene they were filming before us was running longer than expected. The director for the scene, Christian Owen knew I had to be out of the studio no later than 7:30 to get to Nob Hill to do my show, so I knew regardless of when we started shooting, we were definitely pressed for time either way. Soon 2:30 turned to 3:30, and before I knew it, it was close to 5:00. I began to panic because I knew there was no way we were going to film this scene in less than two and a half hours. Being pressed for time and stressed was not going to help my erection.

Marc started to sense my panic. Hot House was a big name in the gay porn industry, and they always produced a quality product with beautiful men. On the other hand, filming with them often took many hours to get the lighting right, and they would sometimes do many takes of one position, which would make the shooting process last even longer than most other studios.

Eventually we started around 5:00. The scene was for a leather movie called *Sektor 9,* and Marc and I were decked out in some really hot fetish gear. I loved the leather scene in the gay community, and it was always one of my goals in my porn career to do a hot leather movie with a big-name studio and a beautiful costar wearing sexy fetish gear. Here I was finally shooting such a, but because we were pressed for time and I was stressed beyond belief, none of that mattered. I was a total mess.

Marc looked at me throughout the shoot and would smile, and I could see he was trying to get me through this and help me calm down. We were both trying really hard to focus on each other and make the scene look hot. We somehow managed to do the scene within the two and a half hours, even though I felt like it was a complete mess and probably one of my weakest pieces of work ever.

Immediately after we came, I jumped in the shower, packed up, and headed to Nob Hill to dance my two shows. That night I packed up my stuff from the theater and drove back to my hotel, where I crawled into bed and tried my best to get some well-needed rest.

The following day I was scheduled to do a live webcam show with another huge name in the porn industry, Spencer Reed. He and I had worked together one time before, but it was for a group scene for Titan, and the only interaction we had had was him pissing on me. We had really wanted to fuck in the scene, but the director for Titan decided it would be best if Trenton Ducati and I fucked and Dario Beck and Spencer paired up. Spencer and I had felt a little disappointed we didn't get to have direct contact with each other, so we were thinking this scene was going to make up for that experience.

The live webcam show was for Raging Stallion Studios, and the directors were Steve Cruz and Bruno Bond. They were a gay couple who had both been pretty big names in the industry, and now they filmed and directed content for Raging Stallion Studios and Falcon. Tonight's shoot was a live webcam series called *Hard Friction*, and the shoots didn't generally last very long. This type of shoot involved some still photography, chatting with fans watching the live broadcast, and filming extra content for the DVD. As soon as we started the still photography, Spencer and I immediately got into each other. He always seemed to have a thing for blonds and I always gravitated toward big hairy daddy types, even though I'm pretty sure Spencer is a few years younger than I am. When he started porn he was young, boyish-looking, and thin, but now he was this huge muscled daddy thanks to a few years of steroids and the rapidly aging lifestyle of a porn star. I didn't care, though, because he looked better as a daddy, and I was ready to be pummeled, fucked, torn up, and used as his bottom boy.

The shoot went well, and Spencer and I had great chemistry. We made a lot of eye contact and had an intense connection I hadn't felt in many of the other scenes I had shot. Spencer fucked me until he was ready to cum, and then he dumped his load in my mouth and I came soon after. Raging Stallion liked a lot of cum and spit play, so we really got into licking up every last drop of our loads and spitting it back and forth into each other's mouths. Spencer, like myself, was a total pig, and we both loved every minute of it. After the shoot was over, I drove Spencer back to his place and then drove back to the hotel.

Yet again, I crawled into my bed and to get some rest before my scene with Titan the following day.

I woke up the following morning feeling slightly rested yet not sure I was ready to shoot more porn. I arrived to the studio and saw one of my scene partners David Anthony outside on his phone smoking a cigarette. We smiled at each other as I walked into the building to greet the crew and meet my other scene partner. I said hi to Patrick O'Conner, the casting director (at the time), and hugged one of the owners and directors, Brian Mills, and the cameraman and director, Paul Wilde. Jasun Marks was there videotaping blog content and filming the scene, and he and I had worked together a few times before. Working with Titan was always a good experience, and I liked their filming process.

Eventually my other scene partner, Tibor Wolfe, came in and we introduced ourselves and began filling out the model release forms. David Anthony came in from smoking and introduced himself to us. He looked at me and said, "Oh, I had no idea you were a model. When I saw you outside I thought you worked in the office upstairs." He kind of chuckled. "I thought to myself that you were cute and you should definitely do porn!".

I smiled at him and laughed but thought, *You had no idea who I was? Didn't you read the e-mails they sent that listed your costars?* I always did and was very sure to check out who I would be filming with.

All three of us began filling out the forms and making small-talk. Immediately I noticed there didn't feel like much (if any) connection between the three of us. I thought they were both attractive but felt there was no chemistry. *Oh boy... I hope this isn't a disaster,* I thought.

The scene with the three of us was going to be a double-penetration scene. They had chosen David because he had a very large dick that pointed upward; he would be the guy on the bottom fucking Tibor. They told me they chose me because of my long legs and big enough dick, so I would be standing up with my legs straddling David, fucking Tibor from behind.

Immediately as Brian Mills tried to orchestrate the entire thing and we began to go through the scene, I felt a little confused. It wasn't rocket science, but filming a double-penetration scene could be difficult and hard to coordinate. The scene took place in an auto garage, and for some reason I didn't have the money to pay David Anthony for his services so (naturally) I got on my knees and sucked his dick to repay him for his hard work. Eventually Tibor (who I assumed also worked at this auto-body shop) saw us fucking and came in began to get double-fucked. Typical porno scenario.

I still didn't feel any chemistry on my part, and I wasn't sure if it was because I was just exhausted or because I had already jinxed myself by saying I was going to fail or what, but the scene was not working for me from the start. To get hard, I tried to think about my hottest porn with big hairy muscled daddies, but that didn't work. I tried to have some play time with both Tibor and David, but that didn't work either. During the shoot, everyone would have to wait for me to get hard, then I would double-fuck Tibor for anywhere from twenty to thirty seconds, stop because I would lose the hard-on, and then we'd have to wait for me to get hard again.

I have to admit that David and Tibor were both incredibly patient and professional in the whole process and waited for me all day to keep getting hard. The shoot lasted from about 11:00 to 6:00 (with a lunch break), and we somehow managed to get through it. I tried my best not to apologize profusely, even though I was upset with my performance and pissed off it hadn't gone well. As soon as we were done I was so relieved. I now had two days to myself before my next shoot for Titan with Johnny Hazzard.

I felt good about the next shoot before I even got to the studio on Thursday morning. I was rested, hadn't shot a load in two days, and knew my scene partner was hot. Johnny Hazzard was a big name in the porn industry and had been filming content for about nine years. We met at the Titan studio and he seemed fairly nice, although he appeared to be over the entire shoot before it even began. Johnny had been doing porn back in a time when models were still being paid two to three thousand dollars a scene (or more), working with the biggest names in the industry and all over every print magazine (back when there was such a thing) and on tons of websites. His name and gay porn went hand in hand. But now he just seemed over it and acted as if he didn't want to be there. We made small-talk, and I tried to get a reading from him, but I had no clue what to think. He kept bitching about Jasun Marks following him around and asking him questions for the Titan blog, and he complained to me about the scene rate we were getting (which was much lower than either of us had anticipated). He also rolled his eyes at everything that anyone on the set said. He was hot, but clearly he didn't want to be there filming with me. I couldn't tell if he just wasn't into me or if it had nothing to do with me, but I tried not to read into it too much.

The scene we did took barely four hours. Generally Titan would take a full day to shoot, but everything went well and we made great time, so we were out of there by early afternoon.

After we were finished and cleaned up, Jasun asked us if he could ask us a few questions for the Titan website blog and for a separate blog. I was always excited to do behind-the-scenes interviews and enjoyed the interaction with fans, but Johnny wanted no part of it. After some pleading, he begrudgingly agreed but rolled his eyes when Jasun wasn't looking. His answers to Jasuns' questions were short, and he clearly wanted to get the fuck out of there and on to wherever he was headed next. I, on the other hand, always loved an opportunity to talk about myself, so I enjoyed every minute of it. We finally wrapped it up and I was on my way back to my hotel to pack for my trip home the next day.

That evening I headed down to the Castro to do some last-minute shopping at a few stores, and then headed to the Powerhouse Bar, where the bartenders got me completely drunk on whiskey and beer. I ended up meeting porn star Tony Vega that night, and we had a fun time together. We both got drunk, and then went back to my place to fuck around. I barely got any sleep and had to wake up early to head back to Vegas.

When I got back the following day, I was happy to be home and spent the first twenty minutes cuddling with the dogs on the couch. I had never been gone so long, so one of the dogs (I'm still unsure which one) had peed all over the sofa when I came in the door. In spite of that, it was definitely great to be home.

After I had some cuddle time with the pups I took a nap. Then I foolishly went out and partied all night with my friends who I hadn't seen in almost two weeks. My friend Jay got locked out of his apartment and needed a place to stay, so he and I ended up hooking up at my place.

I had somehow booked three clients the following day, and knew I needed to see each one of them and live up to my agreeing to see them. I was still tired, feeling a bit run down, and wasn't sure how I was going to be able to get through three sessions when I was running on a few hours of drunken sleep.

I hadn't gotten off for almost two days, although I had that drunken hookup with porn star Tony Vega my last night in San Francisco, and then the other hookup the following night, with my friend Jay. I didn't get off either time because I was so exhausted and drunk and all I wanted to do was just pass out. Both times all we did was make out, roll around, and cuddle. So there was definitely a massive sperm buildup going on in my dick, and I was horny. Generally, being with a client doesn't really do it for me because it's work and I'm trying to focus on their needs and what they want. Having two "almost hookups" and not cumming for a few days was leaving me very sexually frustrated and antsy, so I was hoping at least one of the clients would be hot and I'd have good sexual chemistry with him.

I went to Circus Circus to see my first client, Derrick. He was from Oregon, came to Vegas a few times a year, and I had been seeing him for over a year now. He was an incredibly nice and generous man who loved to spoil me, even though he always managed to stay in the shittiest hotels on the strip. Seeing him was enjoyable but exhausting at the same time. The actual anal penetration with him lasted less than two minutes, but everything leading up to that was too rough, far too aggressive, and physically uncomfortable for me.

He was someone who was enthralled with the porn industry. He would sit there and ask me question after question about it and listen intently as I told him about all my adventures. He treated me like a star, which I found amusing. He kind of looked like he could have been a porn star from the '70s with his moustache—now saggy and slightly stained with tobacco—tighty-whities underwear, and gold chains. We would generally talk for about an hour, and then he would excuse himself to go to the bathroom and would come back to begin the foreplay.

It was kind of obvious to me that he probably watched far too much porn for many years because the way he had sex was similar to how bad porn would happen. He would say a lot of "Oh, yeah, you fucking like it when I drill your little pussy boy butthole?" or "You fucking like that tongue in your little pink asshole, bitch?" Honestly... who really says that? It's not romantic, it's far too aggressive, and to be honest, I found it a little demeaning.

But like a good escort, I moaned back, "Oh, fuck, yeah, Derrick... eat my pink butthole," and moan like it's the best feeling ever.

Eventually, he started to ram his fingers up my ass without lubrication and only a little bit of spit. I tried to endure it for as long as possible, and made sure my face wasn't reading how I really felt. Having a little finger action in my ass wasn't always a bad thing, but what many men do not realize is that the fingernails need to be trimmed and not jagged, there needs to be a lot of lube or spit, and the best thing to do is go slowly and not ram your finger in there like you're frantically ringing a doorbell. Derrick did this for a few minutes and it felt awful. Eventually I acted like it was slightly uncomfortable, as if to say, "Okay, that's enough... let's move on, babe," and we did.

He took the bottle of old-school KY jelly from the nightstand, put on a Trojan, and wrapped up his five-inch cock covered in gray wiry pubic hair that has probably never been trimmed. He flipped me onto my stomach and prepared me to get fucked doggy-style. Personally, I think doggy-style is painful and—like its name—reminds me of two dogs in heat. It's not a pretty position, and it just feels like I am getting rammed from behind. How does this feel good to the bottom? Derrick has always loved this position, and it somehow worked for me because instead of looking at him, I could watch the porn on the screen, make a to-do list in my head, think about the sushi I am going to order from Kaizen Sushi later that night, and block out whatever is happening behind me.

He started off slowly and began to drill my ass. Not only is doggie style uncomfortable, most guys think it works if you just slip it in and start darting your penis in and out. Yet again... some guys are clueless to how this whole "sex" thing works.

"Aw, yeah... baby, you like that huge cock inside you?"

"Fuck, yeah, Derrick... it feels so fucking good."

"Yeah? You love it in your tight boy pussy, don't you?"

"Yes, Derrick... harder, please... HARDER!" I yelled. I knew the more I yelled and acted like it's the best feeling ever, the more he was going to get off. He continued to nail me like a jackhammer and shove my face in the pillow. I tried to get a little peak at the porn on TV as an escape, and he finally shot his load. He continued to pump away as he collapsed on my back.

"Fuck, yeah, baby... that was amazing," he told me.

"Oh, my God, that was so good," I said. We lay there for a few minutes until I finally roll him off my back.

I excused myself to go to the bathroom and take a shower. I had only twenty-five minutes until my next appointment.

I left Circus Circus to drive over to the Venetian. The hotels were not far from each other, but it was Saturday night, and traffic was a nightmare no matter where you were on the Las Vegas Strip. I made it to the Venetian and texted my next client to tell him I was there. His name was Michael and we planned for him to meet me at the bottom of the elevators to "escort" me up to his room because security checked everyone's room key.

I was standing off to the side at the bottom of the elevators. Waiting for a client, especially one I didn't know, was the most uncomfortable feeling for me. I didn't care if people knew I was an escort—I was not the only one in this town doing it—but I felt like a complete hooker waiting for a client in the lobby of a hotel.

As I waited for Michael, I pretended to look at stuff on my phone, but my eyes were glued to everyone coming out of the elevators. Eventually out walked a large black man who made direct eye contact with me, and I realized this was him. Michael was someone I had seen before, but for some reason I had not saved his number in my phone. This really annoyed me, because if I had saved his number, I would not have known not to see him again. He was a very large man with a lot of extra foreskin and a very large belly. The sex was extra work for me, trying to work with his large body and small dick. Before he showed up, part of me was desperately hoping this client and I would have a good chemistry, but when I saw him, I realized what I was in store for. My goal and hope for an encounter with a client isn't that he is necessarily hot or good-looking. I have no expectations the guy will look like a super model. If this were the case, I would not be doing what I was doing. But at the very least, I'm always hoping for a good chemistry between the guy and me.

Michael was a very nice man from Miami, but unfortunately I felt no chemistry with him. I also recalled that he got far too rough with me last time, and I didn't enjoy myself at all. The sex was uncomfortable and at times painful, and I would count down the minutes until I could leave. He got into bondage, whipping, paddling my ass, finger fucking me, and flogging. These are things I sometimes enjoy, but I didn't with him.

There was no turning back now—he had seen me and I had seen him. I turned my disappointment into sheer excitement and said, "Oh, my God... hi!" Sometimes, the only way I could fake how I was really feeling was to transform my feelings of disappointment and exhaustion into sheer and utter excitement and giddy happiness. I had to constantly remind myself that escorting was not a dating service, and I was obliged to do my job and bring some enjoyment and relief to these men. I knew some escorts who will turn and walk away if they get a client who is unattractive or who they don't want to deal with. I know some escorts that have literally gotten up during the session, taken the money on the table, and just walked out because, as they have said, "I don't fuck old guys, ugly dudes, or fat asses." I also knew a few veteran escorts who required clients to submit photos of themselves prior to meeting them so they could choose whether or not to see them. These were escorts who were generally not too concerned with customer service, repeat clients, or people bad-mouthing them on the escorting blogs. I, on the other hand, still had a heart—believe it or not—and always tried to make the best of every situation with a client, although some men had posted things about me on websites and blogs saying I didn't seem like I was "into them" and that there was no chemistry between us during our session. I realized it was all a part of the job, and there was no point in dwelling on it.

Michael and I headed upstairs in the elevator, and as we made small-talk, I was reminded of everything we did last time and how much I really didn't want to be there. He opened the door to his massive suite and I walked in. Sure enough, right beside his bed, he had already laid out whips, nipple clamps, floggers, handcuffs, blindfolds, lube, condoms, paddles, and a plethora of other sex toys I had no interest in using.

Michael was the type of guy that liked a little bit of small-talk, but he was definitely focused on using that full hour to fuck me and get the most out of his session. He was obviously organized with his assortment of toys and props, and I was hoping to avoid using all of them.

We talked about what he was in town for, all that he had done, the various restaurants he had eaten at, and when he was heading back to Miami. He excused himself to go to the rest room and I took off my clothes to get it started. I only had an hour or so until my next client and I wanted to wrap this one up as soon as I could. All I could think about was my sushi and bottle of wine waiting for me at the end of the night and my comfy bed I was going to crawl into.

He came out of the bathroom and I was lying there in my underwear waiting for him to join me. He hopped on the bed, and as it rocked back and forth, I immediately had visions of the whole thing collapsing with us both on it. He went on and on about how gorgeous I was and how he had been looking forward to this for weeks now. He went in to kiss me and I reciprocated. He wanted to do a lot of kissing, and I always agree to kiss because I know a lot of the men get into it, but after a while I try to move onto something if I'm not enjoying it. Kissing is very intimate and I know many escorts won't do it. I, on the other hand, knew that more men wanted kissing and making out more than actual penetration, so I generally always agreed to let them kiss me. Michael liked big, sloppy, wet kisses, which really made my stomach turn. We kissed for a little bit, and he was trying to force as much spit into my mouth and lick around my lips and shove his tongue down my throat. After a few minutes, I gave him my neck as I threw my head back and moaned in ecstasy. I felt as if guys liked that because it affirmed them as good lovers, but it was also an easy way to transition on to something else. Going down on him was always a lot of work and I had to prepare myself for it and keep my eyes closed. His large belly and extra foreskin required work to push back the belly while sucking on his dick and keeping the foreskin back. He really got into it and I tried to do the best oral so I could to wrap this up. After a couple of minutes into it, he told me to suck his balls, and I went down to try to find them but had little luck. He was so large and his balls were so small they got lost in his scrotum and the fat surrounding it. I didn't even know what I was licking.

"Aw, yes, son... yes, son... that's it. Get those big black balls nice and wet, son... Yes, son, you like my big balls?" he asked as he shoved my head into his crotch even harder and I struggled to breathe. All I could smell was the stench of this man's crotch and the cocoa butter he must have lathered on his balls and legs before I got there. It took a lot for me not to throw up.

"That's it, suck on those balls, boy," he moaned. What balls was he talking about? I was licking skin, but there was nothing that looked or felt like balls, but if it felt good for him and he was getting off, then I was fine with it. *Let's just get this over with... I'm tired, horny, and incredibly hungry.* I don't know where my mind was, but I was just trying to do enough to him so he knew I was at least half awake and still doing something down there to keep him entertained.

"FUCK YEAH, SON... lick those big black balls...get 'em nice and wet. SPIT ON 'EM, BOY! You like Daddy's big black nut sack, don't you?" he yelled and grabbed my head to bring my face further into his balls. I take his hands to release them from my head as if to say, "Back off a little bit... that's too rough." He released the pressure, apologized, and continued to grind my face.

Oh, dear Lord, let this end. I'm tired and wanna get outta here, I think. We continued with oral for a few minutes until I told him to start working on my ass because, "I really need it bad." He loved to hear this and pulled out and grabbed a condom and a tube of something that looks like lube. He stood up and directed me to get on my knees and turn away so he can fuck me doggy-style. Again, I detest this position, but at least it gave me an escape from whatever business was happening behind me and I could focus on thinking about that rainbow roll, sashimi, and shrimp tempura I was going to be scarfing down later.

He started to rub jelly from a blue tube all over his dick and I reached for it as he put it on the nightstand.

"Is this lube?" I asked.

"No, it's numbing gel. It helps me from cumming too quickly."

"Oh... Great," I said. I was hoping to speed this session up while he was using an ointment to slow it down.

We carried on fucking for about forty-five minutes and I could see that we were way over our time, and I had to get going. He hadn't even used any of the toys he had laid out next to the bed and I was totally fine with that.

"Do you think you can cum?" I asked him.

"Oh, yeah... sure. You want me to hurry up, don't you?"

"No, it's cool, but I just have to get going shortly."

He ended up cumming within the next few minutes, and afterward I got up to shower and head out. I thanked him graciously for calling me and he saw me to the door.

Once outside his room, I saved his number and wrote DO NOT ANSWER next to his name. I head toward the elevators and I'm off and running to appointment number three. I'm still tired, hungry, and oddly horny. There's something intense about having so much sex and not getting off, and it leaves you feeling even hornier and sexually frustrated.

I get to the Bellagio for my last appointment, and texted my client Mark to meet me downstairs by the elevator because, again, security won't let me up without a room key. I waited for a few minutes by the gift shop that faced the bank of elevators and watched the people coming out and heading toward the casino. Every time I saw a hot guy come out of the elevators, I made eye contact with him hoping it was my client. Some of them made eye contact with me, but they all walked right past me toward the casino.

Finally I heard someone beneath me say, "Hiya, Christopher, it's me, Mark!"

I literally had a second where I heard the voice but didn't see a person. Then I looked down. In front of me stood a man no more than five feet tall with a little smile on his face. I'm a little taken aback by how tiny this guy is, and I immediately think, *This is him?*

He extended his hand and said, "Hiya, mate. How you doing?"

"I'm well. You're Mark?" I asked.

"Yes, sir, let's head to my room," and off we went. On the way, he told me he was from England, but spent a lot of time in the U.S. He

130

would be on his way to San Francisco the following day and just had a huge business dinner with friends. We got to the room and stepped inside. It was a beautiful penthouse suite overlooking the Bellagio fountains with an amazing view of the strip. His suite is nice, but there is a half-eaten cart of room service food in the middle of the bedroom, with a half-empty bottle of wine next to it. The room smelled like the food has been sitting there for a while. *Nothing like the stench of smelly room service food to get you in the mood for sex.*

"So I called you here because this is something I've been wanting to try for quite some time," he said.

"Being with an escort?" I asked.

"Well... being with an escort and being with a man. I have never done either."

"Okay, cool. Are you married?"

"No, but I've had a girlfriend for years, and she loves having sex with me and I love fucking her, but I really wanted to try something new. I've been contemplating doing this for a couple years and it took me this long to finally do it. I heard about rentboy.com through a friend at work. He's very wealthy and is a good-looking man who also happens to hire escorts. He told me to give it a go, and I decided to look at the guys available in Sin City. What happens in Vegas stays in Vegas, right?"

"Of course!" I laughed even though I absolutely hated hearing people use that expression. It's an ad campaign that really needs to end because it basically encourages tourists to do whatever they want when they come to Vegas and drive the locals crazy while doing it.

I wanted to prolong the conversation and make the sex go as quickly as possible. It wasn't because Mark was short, but because he looked like a leprechaun and I did not find him at all attractive. He was slightly overweight and wore his pants pulled up over his bellybutton. He had thinning ginger hair with a ginger-colored scraggly beard. I was not looking forward to this, but knew I had to do what I came here to do.

Mark spoke very highly of himself and his "techniques" he used while making love to his girlfriend and he was now ready to share them with men, and he wanted me to be the first to experience them. *Hooray for me.* It felt like he thought I should feel privileged, but instead I was mortified and dreading every minute of it.

"My girl loves it when I fuck her hard. We have the best sex ever, but being with a man is something I've always wanted to try. I've lost over a hundred pounds in the last year or so and I'm feeling good about my body and think it'd be fun to mess around with a man." I was taken aback by how confident and sure of himself this guy is. He was oddly confident for an overweight, short, homely person.

He told me to make myself more comfortable and relax on the bed. He became quiet as he undressed. He took off his shirt and I saw that he was covered in ginger body hair from head to toe, front to back, with rolls of excess skin from all the weight he lost. Seeing a person's body after they have lost over 100 pounds can be scarier than seeing a 450-pound-man undress. He tried to be very seductive and sexy as he removed every article of clothing he was wearing. I cringed on the inside but smiled like I love it and told him to take it all off.

After his strip show he lay on the bed next to me, and asked me to remove my clothes. As I did so, I checked out his midsection and noticed he has giant flaps of skin hanging down and covering his penis. I tried to make a plan as to how I would move that around when we get started.

"Wow, your body is amazing, Christopher."

"Thanks, babe," I said to him as I smile. He touched my body, starting from my face to my thighs. I still hadn't cum yet, and I had already taken one and half Viagra that night, so my dick was rock hard. He went in to grab my dick and he could barely wrap his tiny hands around my shaft. It was kind of impressive how big my dick looked in his small hands.

He stroked me for a few minutes, then looked at me and asked, "Can I suck it?"

"Sure, go for it," I said and he moved his head in closer to it. He looked up at me with excitement and a bit of apprehension.

"Okay, here goes nothing," he said, before putting it in his mouth. Poor little guy could barely get the head of it in his tiny mouth, but he took it like a champ and continued to suck on it and lick it like a lollipop. As he went down on me, I couldn't help but wonder if he was as excited about sucking my dick as I was the first time I sucked cock in high school when I was fourteen years old and went down on my best friend. The first time I sucked cock I remember thinking I was about to do something I had only dreamt about for years, and the sheer excitement of that made my dick want to explode without even touching myself.

He continued giving me oral sex until I couldn't handle the scraping of his teeth on my dick any longer. I took his shoulders and brought him in closer to me and gave him a giant kiss.

"Your lips are so soft," he told me.

"Thank you, yours too," I said even though his were dry, chapped, flaky, and scaly.

"Will you go down on me?" he asked and I agreed. I figured it was eventually going to have to happen, so I might as well start now and wrap this up. It was tricky to move around the excess skin hanging around his dick as I went down on him, but I was able to make him feel good somehow. He moaned and acted like it was the best thing ever as he threw his head back. I can't even begin to tell how awful he tasted or smelled, and I tried to not think about it the entire time it was happening. I stomached it for about five minutes until I figured it was time to start with the actual penetration.

"Did you want to fuck me?" I asked.

"Definitely, mate. Do you think you should try fucking me, too?"

"We can try, but to be honest you might want to try starting with something smaller if you've never had anal sex before."

"Sometimes my girlfriend puts a finger in my ass."

"That's hot, and we can totally try, but we only have ten minutes left. Do you want to try fucking me first, and if we have time I'll fuck you?"

"Sure, that sounds good."

I climbed on top of him and put his dick inside of me. As I started riding him, I threw back my head and said, "Fuck, yeah, that's it, Mark." His penis was barely five inches long and covered in excess skin from all the weight he lost. I was skeptical about how well this was going to work, but we continued to go at it. I had to force all the skin back from his stomach to keep his dick inside me, and I tried my best to ride it without letting it fall out.

By this point in my life, I had already bottomed for quite a few large dicks, and my ass wasn't loose or stretched out, but it took a lot of work and coordination to put a small penis inside of me and be penetrated for a period of time. We kept at it for a few minutes, and he seemed to like it and tell me how much tighter it was than his girlfriend's pussy. Time was running out, and he wasn't close to cumming, so I finished him off with a hand job and he came all over himself. I was relieved when it was over and happy to collect my money after I gave myself a silk-wood scrub in the shower.

"Do you travel internationally?" he asked.

"Yes, I do. Why do you ask?"

"I think it'd be great to take you to England with me. I go to London quite often, and I would love to take you with me the next time I go for two weeks."

"That would be amazing. I love London," I told him as I secretly prayed he would never call me again. I could barely stomach an hour with him, let alone two weeks playing the role of boyfriend and having sex every day.

"I'm going to check my schedule and get back to you. I definitely want to set it up with you. How much would you charge?"

"About fifteen hundred dollars a night," I lied. It was usually about a thousand a night, and I'm always willing to work with someone on a long-term type of arrangement, but there wasn't enough money in the world to get me to see this man again.

"Oh, that's not a problem. We'll be in touch."

He wrapped his tiny arms around my waist and gave me a giant hug, and I left his suite and walked toward the elevator, ready to drag my tired ass home after I stopped to get my sushi. But first I put Mark's number in my phone as "Mark from UK. Never answer or see him again," and hit save.

In the elevator, I had to keep readjusting my dick in my underwear because it was still rock-hard from all the. I saw in my messages that a guy named Alex had sent me a text message. He was a guy I had hooked up with a few times before and he was always texting me to meet again. He wasn't bad-looking, but the sex wasn't amazing and I remember the last time we fucked had been messy because he hadn't douched properly. I realize after having a lot of sex in my lifetime this happens quite often, but when you have sex for a living, having mediocre sex with a guy you really weren't into all that much—and it being pretty messy—wasn't something you wanted to do again unless you were really horny and needed to get laid. I guess tonight was one of those nights, because I was really horny and I had a giant hard-on that needed to be tended to. He asked me if I wanted to come over and I said sure, and was on my way. His apartment was a few minutes away from my favorite sushi place, so I figured it would be killing two birds with one stone. Sex and sushi, then I'll be on my way home to relax and drink a bottle of wine.

When I got to his apartment, I saw the keys were in the handle and the door was slightly open. I figured this was his invitation for me to come in and find him face first in his pillow with his ass up in the air, ready to get fucked. Instead, I opened the door, which directly faced the bathroom, and saw him scrubbing his ass with a washcloth in front of the sink. He saw me, screamed, and slammed the door.

"Hey, Alex, I'm sorry. I didn't mean to freak you out. Your keys were in the door and the door was open. I figured you were home and that meant it was okay for me to come in."

He laughed nervously behind the bathroom door. "It's okay. I was just cleaning up," he said over the water running in the background.

His clothes were on the floor, and it seemed as if he had run into the house, stripped off his clothes, and went to the bathroom to clean up and douche. He must have really been in a hurry to get laid. His place smelled like shit and the aroma was lingering throughout the apartment.

God, this was definitely not going as planned, and this night was getting worse by the minute. By this point I didn't even want to have sex anymore, but I figured I was there and he already saw me, so I couldn't be rude and leave. My plan was to fuck him for a few minutes, cum, go get my sushi, head home, and crack open that bottle of Merlot and call it a night.

After a few more minutes of clean-up time, Alex came out of the bathroom wearing a towel. He was ready to go, and I was too. *Let's do this so I can get off and be home.* We went to his bedroom and I climbed onto his bed. He turned on the TV and pressed play on the DVD player. On came some porn with two blond guys in a locker room in some type of jock scene. I never understood watching porn while having sex. *Why would I look at the TV if I have the real thing in front of me?* He started asking me questions about porn stars and who the guys on the screen were. I had no idea and had no interest in finding out. The movie had obviously been filmed anywhere from five to ten years ago and already seemed a bit dated. Although I do porn, I have no clue who half the guys in the industry are, especially the ones from five or more years before I began filming.

Alex climbed into bed and we began making out. He was cute and had soft skin and I liked kissing him. It didn't even matter that he wasn't drop-dead gorgeous or didn't have a huge dick. It was enough that I was not getting paid to have sex, and instead I was having sex with someone because I wanted to and not because they had purchased me for an hour. For some reason, having mediocre sex with average-looking guys was enough to hit the spot sometimes, and I was kind of happy to be there. Alex was a power bottom and climbed on top of my dick and slid it in. We started going at it and continued to get rougher and harder by the minute. We looked at each other as our sexual chemistry intensified and my rock-hard dick was throbbing inside his tight ass. I remembered the one thing he loved was when I fucked him really hard and he would just bounce around on my dick screaming. It was kind of entertaining to watch such a little guy flailing around on top of me, and it made my dick even harder. I reached up to grab his throat and choke him a little bit as I fucked him harder and harder. Cutting off some air drove him even wilder and he screamed even louder. I rammed my cock in, harder and harder, thrusting my hips deep in to his ass. I didn't care about being physically exhausted anymore. I had gotten my second wind and I was having a blast.

Suddenly, he looked at me and my dick slipped out of his ass and flopped back and forth on my thighs. He looked at me horrified and at that second something wet and loose fell out of his ass and all over my legs. We just looked at each other and he said, "Oh, my God, I'm so sorry," and jumped off the bed and ran to the bathroom. "Stay there!" he yelled.

I was scared to look down. I knew exactly what happened, and I didn't want to see what was on my legs. I stared up at the ceiling and said to myself, *This is God's way of punishing you for being such a fucking whore.* I kept my hands away from my legs and refused to touch anything until I had a towel to wipe up the mess. I finally looked down and saw exactly what I had imagined... a chocolate mess from my waist to my knees. *Fuck my life.* In all my years and sexual experiences, I had never had anyone get so messy on me... a term some might call "Painted."

Alex ran back in with a towel, and I used it to wipe everything off me, then went to the bathroom to get further cleaned up. He was mortified and I tried my best to brush it off as no big deal. The last thing I wanted to do was leave an emotional scar on this kid and keep him from bottoming again. He had a nice fat tight Latin ass he needed to share with the world, and I kind of felt embarrassed for him. Being a gay man that has sex for a living, I was used to "messy situations," although this was the first time someone had completely relieved himself on me.

I turned on the shower, and he continued to apologize profusely. To change the subject, I asked him about his job and how his dogs were. As we were making small-talk and I was waiting for the water to warm up, I caught a glimpse of myself in the bathroom mirror. I was standing there, naked, covered in shit, afraid to touch anything. I began to smile and then started to laugh at the humor in it all. This was definitely a turning point when I realized I needed to write a book because these odd situations were becoming too much to keep to myself. I cleaned up in the shower and gave myself another silk-wood scrub with almost the entire bottle of Axe body wash that was sitting on a shelf. The smell of feces was next to impossible to get out, and I was not going to go light on the soap. I was hoping he maybe even had some Windex or Clorox spray in the bathroom to use on my hands, because there was no way I wanted to smell that stench as I ate my rainbow roll later that night.

I finished cleaning up, got dressed, and we continued to make small-talk as I collected my belongings. When he asked if I still wanted to get off, I smiled and thought about it. My dick was still hard and it probably wouldn't go down until I came, so I said sure. I lay back down on the bed where he had accidentally taken a shit on me ten minutes before and began stroking my cock. He stood on the floor and jerked off as I sucked his balls. Within a few minutes he came all over my face, which immediately prompted me to shoot my load all over my stomach. Not at all how I envisioned my night to be, but it was better than nothing, and I had finally shot the load that had been hoping to get out all night.

Once again, I got cleaned up in the bathroom, dressed, and collected my stuff to go. We hugged and I left to get my sushi. Within two minutes my phone was blowing up with apologetic, embarrassed texts from him. At that point, I knew I never wanted to see him again. Nice kid, cute ass, but what had just happened sealed the deal. I knew I would have to find a new fuck buddy on the side.

I drove to Kaizen sushi only to learn they had closed early that night. I nearly burst into tears. All I wanted was sushi and edamame, and I felt defeated and like the world was against me. I drove to the grocery store and picked up some odd-looking sushi and seaweed salad from the deli. I had my mind set on sushi, and I figured it was either that or a frozen burrito.

I went home, cracked open the bottle of Merlot, and began eating the seaweed salad. It was absolutely disgusting and I spit it into a napkin. I tried some of the rainbow roll and California roll, but they were equally bad. I finished about three pieces of sushi and the entire bottle of wine and climbed into bed.

The next morning, I woke up with the worst stomachache ever, and I literally went to the bathroom seventeen times that day. I had liquids coming out of both ends of my body, and I had to crawl from my bed to the toilet all day. I had never felt so awful before and had no idea what made me so sick. It could have been all the traveling, the drinking two nights before, or one of my clients might have been ill, or it could have been the horrendous sushi I ate before bed, or the $1.99 bottle of emergency Merlot I downed before I passed out. After being in bed for nearly eighteen hours, I asked my ex-boyfriend Patrick to come over that night. He made me tea and watched a movie with me. I didn't feel better for almost seven days, and I ended up losing ten pounds that week. I went to the doctor, and the only thing he saw when he did some tests were that my white blood cells were low. Everything else was normal, and I just needed time to recover. I didn't escort, have sex, or drink for eight days. I missed out on making a lot of money that week and a few good parties, but I didn't care. My body needed a break and I welcomed the time off.

Chapter Eleven

Dating an Escort

People often ask me if I have a boyfriend. The answer to that is simple... no. Dating as an escort or porn star can be complicated, and while some are able to do it without any problems—apparently these guys exist, like unicorns—at this point in my life it's not what I could handle.

I think I spent a majority of my life wanting a partner, husband, caregiver, and best friend who would be there for me at all times. Even when I was going through ex-gay therapy, I would dream of being married to a woman and having daily companionship with someone. I imagined being in a committed partnership, and it excited me. Of course, when I was fantasizing about this woman—like any other repressed narcissistic homosexual—I would be thinking about how beautiful our wedding would be, her Vera Wang gown, and how handsome I would look in my fitted tuxedo.

I had these delusional visions throughout my twenties, and I would say, even while I loved and still love Patrick, our relationship was not at all stable, committed, or healthy. After we broke up, I spent a few months on my own, and I was so preoccupied with buying the house and starting this new business of escorting that I didn't have time to consider a relationship.

Eventually I started dating a guy I met through mutual friends named Spencer Williams. Spencer was nice, and I think he was just what I needed at the time. He helped me with the transition of getting over the relationship I had been in and into a new life as a gay man in my late twenties. After ten months of dating on and off, I realized it was time to move on. I had been dating him for the wrong reasons. Again, I wanted to be with someone who would fulfill needs that were not being met within myself and I was looking toward him to do that. He always did the best he could, and we enjoyed our time together, but the entire relationship felt forced on my part and not quite what I was looking for or needed. While I cared for him and enjoyed our time together, we were on two separate pages.

Shortly after we broke up, Spencer met someone new and began dating him. I, on the other hand, felt like it was time to be single and was still dealing with my breakup with Patrick and, now, with Spencer. In my mind, I knew it was time to get used to being on my own, although there was still a huge part of me that craved to be in a relationship.

I first noticed Jason Michaels on rentboy.com. We had ads running at the same time, and they were next to each other on the website. Instantly, I was drawn to his ad and looked at his pictures almost every week I visited the site. He was so beautiful, he took my breath away. I had been escorting for a while and had been hired out with other guys from the website on several different occasions. I kept hoping Jason and I would be hired out together so I could at least meet him and maybe even have sex with him. Surprisingly, the time came, but during the meeting with the client, Jason and I had little to no interaction with each other, and I left feeling a little disappointed and sexually frustrated.

About six months later, he showed up at my gym. I belonged to a privately owned Crossfit gym, and the only time non-members were allowed to come in and do the workouts was once a month during a three-day open-gym period. During this time, family and friends of members could try out the workouts and see if Crossfit Training was something they wanted to do.

I came into the gym one day in July when it was at least 110 degrees outside and the gym looked packed. Class sizes were generally kept small with no more than twenty people, but there were at least thirty there that day. I spotted Jason immediately. Suddenly I became shy and acted as if I didn't know him. I wanted to smile and say hi, but the only thing I could think of to say was, "Hi, remember me? The last time I saw you was when we were doing awkward things with a client together in a hotel room." Instead, I just started warming up and talking to a few friends I had in the class.

I left the gym that day and didn't see Jason until one evening the following September, when we were both on a popular hookup site. It was the first time I ever saw him on there and was unsure if I should say anything. The options of men on the site were slim to none, and I generally spent my time trolling around just looking at other guys' pictures to pass the time. I figured I might as well say hi and get it over with. It was easier to do it online than in person, so I typed him a message that simply read, "Hi." He responded and we ended up spending the next few hours chatting back and forth. Eventually we met up for dinner later that week and started dating soon after.

My relationship with Jason brought up a lot of anger, frustration, depression, and sadness in me. For some unknown reason, I was in love with the guy from the moment I saw his pictures online. I guess it was love at first sight, but that doesn't mean it was a healthy or a sustaining love.

There was something about him—his tanned skin, his muscular, hairy body—that made me melt. It was almost as if looking at him made me feel like he was everything I wasn't or would never be. I felt gangly and tall, skinny, pale, and average. Jason was beautiful and exotic, and something inside me wanted him more than I could even handle.

As we started seeing each other, I began to fall more and more in love with him. Deep down inside, I knew I wasn't just "falling" in love with him because I was actually in love with him. I desperately wanted to be loved by him, but I had absolutely no self-confidence in myself. In him, I saw everything I was not. I felt unattractive, inadequate, and passed by, whereas—to me—he stood out and people always noticed him when he stepped in the room. I felt he had the pure physical beauty I desired to have.

As the months went on and we continued dating, I came to realize there was little to nothing to sustain the relationship, but I refused to give up on it and wouldn't call it quits without putting up a fight. I was determined to make it work because he fulfilled everything I was looking for in a partner physically, we had a good time together, and I was scared of being alone. Weren't those reasons—plus a little hard work—enough to sustain a relationship? Obviously the answer is no, but I was stubborn, and I refused to let go. Also, as an escort and porn star, finding someone who is accepting of what you do can be incredibly difficult, and sometimes it was easier to date someone else in the industry who did the same thing as you, even if it created feelings of jealousy, resentment, and tension.

We tried to have balance and continue escorting and doing porn, but our relationship was basically doomed before it even began. In my mind, I thought, *If only we could balance escorting and doing porn, and focus on being there for each other, then we could have a healthy and a happy relationship.*

I was ready to fight tooth and nail for it because being happy with someone else meant that I could truly be happy within myself. I wanted love, acceptance, and great sex from him, adoration from clients and fans, but it never seemed to click. We continued dating for a few months until I somehow slipped into a deep depression that I couldn't shake. I didn't want to keep going with the relationship, and I was exhausted trying to make something work that was clearly not going to. I had tried sharing myself and sharing him by doing porn and escorting, but I knew it couldn't last and I was not happy doing it.

Patrick used to tell me I always wanted to have my cake and eat it too, and I never argued with him when he said it. I would act offended and pout about it, but we both knew it was true and there was no point in fighting the truth.

I did want to be in a relationship with Jason, but I also wanted to continue escorting for the money and do porn for the fame. I wanted him there for the daily approval I desperately needed from someone.

Within the past decade, I had gone from questioning my sexuality to spending a few years on cruise ships where I slept around and had a few relationships. Eventually I met Patrick, and even though I barely knew him, I essentially got married to him within a few months. Before he had come along, I basically had been in the closet and hadn't had much experience dating anyone. After our relationship crumbled, I took a few months off and then jumped into a new relationship with Spencer, and when that ended, I took another few months off before picking up my dysfunctional patterns with Jason. I didn't want to pay attention to the fact that Jason was eight years younger than I was, had little to no ambition in his own personal life, spent every day smoking weed, and would generally drink half a bottle of tequila and get sloppy drunk before we would go out. At the time, none of it mattered because all I could see was his physical and sexual beauty. I was attracted to him, and I had an overwhelming need to be loved. Deep down he was a good guy and always tried his best to make our relationship work, but I had eight years on him and knew that I wanted something more than what I had with him.

When it became clear that neither one of us could handle all the different, dysfunctional aspects of the relationship; I knew it was time to end it. We spent nearly an entire year and a half after the initial breakup fighting, getting back together, breaking up again, making up, breaking up, having random drunken hookups at 4 a.m., and making an occasional late-night phone call in which we would spend an hour or so screaming at and telling each other how one was ruining the other's life and we never wanted to speak to each other again. It was all very dramatic (to say the least), but for some reason our relationship had a strong hold on us both and neither one of us had an easy time breaking it off with the other.

I realize now it was necessary to go through all of this so I could finally be totally and completely okay with being alone and on my own, which is something I continue to work on. I was tired of trying to find approval and acceptance from the men I was dating, and I finally came to a place where I realized I might never be with someone else, especially while I was pursuing porn and living the life of an escort. Rather than be upset with that thought, I took comfort in it because I knew it was time for the healing to begin and to be okay with being on my own. This is all very basic, of course, and when I was finally able to come to terms with it, there was a part of me that thought, *Well, obviously, Christopher*. It may seem simple, but this life lesson was teaching me that it was time to start taking responsibility for myself. I still struggle with this because there is a huge part of me that craves daily companionship and intimacy with someone else. I had always felt little connection to my family and I would consider only a small group of people to be close friends, so I had been trying to get those needs met in a partner, and it was not happening, perhaps because I had yet to learn to be happy on my own.

Even knowing this about myself, I still find myself falling for the wrong guys simply because they are making themselves available to me and I figure it's worth a try. and maybe I can make love happen. It's amazing the things we try to convince ourselves to do or think, but I believe many of us do this on some level. I am trying to at least recognize this when I find myself doing it and end it before I get too invested and its becomes harder and harder to get out.

Chapter Twelve

Even Escorts Get the Blues

The week after Jason and I broke up—for the first time—I went to Long Beach for four days. We had planned the trip a few months earlier, seeing it as a time to get away from the city, turn off our phones, and not see clients. After the break-up, I decided to make use of the trip, seeing as I couldn't get a refund from the hotel. I figured I might as well enjoy a few days in Long Beach with a hotel room overlooking the ocean and the *Queen Mary* parked next to me. I welcomed the time on my own and figured it would be good to relax, maybe see a few clients, and have some downtime to think.

The evening I arrived, I was able to settle into my room, but I had to shower and get changed quickly because I had a client coming over around 11 p.m. The man's name was Jesse, and although he was nervous, he was very nice and we had a relaxed time together for a little over an hour.

After he left, I jumped in the shower to rinse off. I wanted to head out to the gay area of Long Beach, where all the bars and nightclubs were, to have a drink. It was only a Thursday night, but I figured something would be going on at one of the bars. I drove down and began to look for parking but was unsuccessful. I literally drove around the area with all the gay bars for almost an hour but was out of luck. I could not believe it, as it was a weeknight and the clubs looked only somewhat busy, yet there was not a single parking spot in site. How do people live in Long Beach deal with this parking nightmare?

I finally said screw it and began looking for another gay bar that was out of this area. The only one I could find was called Pistons, and it was about eleven miles away. I drove down there and saw there were very few cars around the bar, but at least there was parking. At this point I didn't care and I just needed a drink. After I parked next to the building, I walked into an empty bar with a bartender who looked to be about seventy years old. I asked for a beer, and he gave me a plastic cup of about eight ounces of beer for six dollars. Kind of a rip–off, but I said thank you and figured I might as well relax for a few minutes before heading back to the hotel. The bartender didn't really seem like he wanted to make conversation, so I sat in silence and looked around. It was one of the dingiest bars I had ever been to. I love going to hole-in-the-wall types of bars, but this place was just depressing. I wanted to finish my overpriced beer and get back to my hotel to go to bed.

When I finally got back to my room, I brushed my teeth, took off my clothes, and climbed into bed, listening to the ocean outside my window. I was tired from the drive down and was still feeling emotionally drained from my breakup with Jason. I was dealing with the heartache, even though I knew it was for the better that we were apart. But I also missed him, and a big part of me wanted him there next to me in bed listening to waves' crash outside the window. I don't know what it was about him or our relationship, but I thought about him constantly, and there was a sadness in my heart I couldn't shake. I fell asleep feeling sad that night and woke up still missing him. Even though I knew it was time for us to move on, it was still nearly impossible not to think of him every other minute of the day.

I spent the following day shopping and driving around Long Beach. I drove back to the local gayborhood and miraculously found a parking spot. I visited the various shops and found the local leather and fetish store, where I bought some new lambskin leather pants. Although they were more than I wanted to spend, I couldn't help it because they were fitted, soft, and felt amazing. I wasn't sure if I could justify spending the money because who actually wears leather pants in the desert where it's scorching hot for a majority of the year. Who cares? I was still feeling heartbroken and needed to do some retail therapy.

I was scheduled to meet a guy named Greg who had contacted me by e-mail a few days ago. We were scheduled to meet at his West Hollywood condo later that afternoon. After I was finished shopping, I packed up my car and began my drive into the city, where I knew I would be fighting rush-hour traffic.

On my way to Greg's, I got a phone call from an L.A. area code. "Hello."

"Hi, is this Christopher?"

"Yes, this is. Who's this?"

"Hi, my name is Dale, and I'm located here in the Hills, and I was wondering if you had any time to meet today?"

"Sure, I could meet you tonight. How about 8 p.m.?"

"Yeah, that works. It would be for my boyfriend and me. I'm in my late forties, good-looking, and my boyfriend is in his early twenties. We were both wondering if you have facial hair right now."

"I don't have a beard. Is that what you were looking for?"

"Yeah, that's fine. I like the beard, but he doesn't, but it's no problem. How much for your time for two guys?"

I was driving and trying to focus on the road, and without thinking about my actual rate I blurted out, "Four hundred dollars," when it was actually five hundred. Oh well... too late now. I guess four hundred would be the rate this time.

"Okay, great. Also, will you be able to top as well as bottom?"

I am versatile, but I generally only bottom when I'm with a client just in case I can't get hard. For some reason, I felt pressured to take this client because I needed the money, so I said, "Yes, I'm versatile."

"Okay, great. I'll text you my address."

"Okay, perfect. See you soon, Dale."

"See you soon," and he hung up.

Three clients in less than three hours? I was not looking forward to this. I could generally do two clients within a few hours of each other, but three within a few hours of each other was going to be pushing it.

I got to Greg's at around 6 p.m. He lived in a beautiful townhouse right in the middle of West Hollywood. The place was newly renovated, and I could tell this guy obviously had money. He was young and pretty cute. He seemed a little nerdish but in an endearing kind of way.

I had taken half a Viagra before I met him, but it hadn't kicked in yet. In fact, I had been pretty much soft for the last few clients I had met that week, but I remained hopeful that it was just a phase and hoped for the best that day. I didn't quite know what the problem was, but I had a pretty good idea it was a psychological problem, not a physical one. After a breakup, I would completely lose my appetite for a few weeks and have to force myself to eat, and I would have little to no sex drive,

149

so getting erect generally was not an option. My heart, mind, and body were all connected, and I couldn't get hard to save my life. I would depend on the erectile dysfunction drugs but knew they weren't always a guarantee. Even though I usually only bottomed with clients, I knew a lot of them liked to see that I was turned on with an erection. Regardless of whether or not I was turned on, I could generally act like I was, and the magical little blue pills always helped convey that illusion.

Thankfully, Greg and I had some chemistry and the pill started kicking in, so I was able to stay hard for most of our time together. I bottomed for him, so it wasn't crucial I remained erect the entire time, and he seemed to enjoy it and was able to get off.

I left his place around 7 p.m. and figured I would need about an hour to find the next place and fight traffic. After wandering the Hollywood Hills for what felt like hours, I finally found Dale's place. I parked my enormous Challenger in his tiny hilled driveway and made my way up to the front door. Dale was waiting by the window of his beautiful home to greet me. He was taller, in his forties, and pretty good-looking. He welcomed me inside, and I stepped into a large foyer with a high ceiling. The foyer had pennies glued to the wall, and it looked really cool. I mentioned how much I liked the pennies idea, and he told me about the tedious process it took to glue them all on one at a time.

He led me into the kitchen and living room, where he was watching a basketball game on TV. I saw two large dogs in the backyard looking inside the house and wishing they could come in.

We made some small-talk while we waited for the boyfriend to come downstairs, and he told me a little bit about the line of work he did and about how long he and his boyfriend had been together.

After a few minutes, a younger guy in his twenties came downstairs and immediately I recognized what kind of relationship they had. Now, don't get me wrong; I don't know either of them, but right away something in my brain screamed out, "SUGAR DADDY" and "mismatch."

"Christopher, this is Roberto. Roberto this is Christopher."

We shook hands, he gave me a half smile, and said hello, but he already looked bored with everything. He had his BlackBerry in his other hand and immediately began looking at it and frantically sending off texts to someone. My assumptions could have been way off, but he reminded me of every other gay guy in West Hollywood I see running around Santa Monica Boulevard who thinks they are far more important than they really are. Clearly, this setup between the two clients was not based on love but on convenience. Dale was older and got to have this younger cute boy to be his lover, and Roberto got to have someone take care of him. Right away, I felt uncomfortable. The small-talk was strained. Roberto acted like he was annoyed with everything that came out of Dale's mouth, like a teenager pissed off with his parent for embarrassing him in front of his friends. Dale asked Roberto if he was okay, and Roberto went off about some drama happening with work and how he was trying to deal with it all, sounding like a hero throughout the entire story. Sometimes West Hollywood gays make me uncomfortable, and I have no idea what to say to them. When I meet them, I generally want to smack them, but I refrain, and I just smile, nod, and try to find someone else to talk to. I find West Hollywood breeds a certain kind of uptight gay who is always on the go, thinks he's famous, lives beyond his means, and wears far too much self-tanner. Roberto looked like he was one their resident ringleaders.

After a few minutes of forced conversation, we made our way upstairs into the large master bedroom. I noticed there was a huge screen on the wall facing the bed, and Dale asked if I minded if they played some porn. I said sure, and he put in a porn I was very familiar with called *Fucking Crazy* from Treasure Island Media.

"Oh, cool. I like this one," I said.

"Yeah, it's pretty hot. We love Treasure Island," Dale said.

I got undressed and positioned myself in the middle of the bed. I figured I was the guest star in the bedroom that night, so I might as well make myself ready for them both. They then began arguing like an old married couple about the lights, the volume of the porn, and other things I found irrelevant to the evening. I felt like I was on a camping trip with my family and listening to my parents argue about meaningless shit after driving in the car all day together. I had taken another half a Viagra and was praying for it to kick in as Dale and Roberto got undressed and settled into the bed next to me.

I looked at Roberto's body, and noticed that he was in good shape. He was wearing a jockstrap, which told me he was ready to get his ass used and abused by us both. Right away, self-doubt began to creep in and something inside me said there was no chance I would be able to get hard for this. I knew from experience that once a tiny bit of self-doubt creeps in, I'm basically fucked. My erections—like most men's—were primarily psychological, and with the combination of my depression from my recent breakup and the bitching going back and forth between Dale and Roberto, I knew this meeting was not going to be what they hoped for. Part of me wanted to just grab my clothes, apologize, and leave, but I felt like things weren't even that bad, so why would I leave? It's not like they were asking me to do things I didn't want to do. But something inside me said this was clearly not going to work, and I might be screwing myself over if I stay.

As I started making out with Dale and caressing his body, Roberto began touching me while begrudgingly kissing Dale just to appease him. I caressed Roberto's body and saw that he has shaved off all of his body and pubic hair. He was covered in a bad case of razor burn and bumps all over his body and especially above his dick area. I prefer body hair on a man, or completely no hair. One of my biggest turn-offs is when a man is hairy but obviously shaves his body and he is left with nothing but red bumps and stubble that hurts when it rubs against my skin. Roberto's razor burn looked uncomfortable and painful, and I was afraid to go near it.

I could tell Roberto is ready and raring to get fucked by me, so I tried to forget about everything going on around me—the uncomfortable arguing, the bumps from his itchy razor burn that's chafing my skin—and I tried desperately to clear my mind of any image or thought of Jason. My head was starting to feel congested from all the Viagra, but it wasn't really enough to sustain a rock-hard erection to fuck Roberto's ass. I zero into the porn where I see a hot guy wearing a jockstrap getting fucked raw by a group of sexually charged aggressive men. The porn was a complete fantasy; I imagined how hot it would be to be able to fuck like the men on the screen with no consequences. To just let as many guys fuck me raw or me fuck an eager blindfolded bottom as he begs for more from the group of men. I tried to create this fantasy in my head to help me get hard, and to my surprise, my dick started to get a little hard after a minute or two. I knew it was either now or never, so I grabbed a condom, greased up my dick, and shoved it into Roberto's ass. Add a condom to an only semi-hard dick, and it wasn't long before my erection was totally dead. I was able to fuck him for a few minutes, but it was definitely not the ass pounding he was begging for. Immediately, I felt like a failure and I continued to tell myself to just leave and forget about it. Who cared if I didn't make any money? Something inside me was telling me to get the fuck out because this was not worth it!

I took my limp dick out of his ass and apologized. I climbed back on the bed and tried to pay attention to Dale so that nobody felt left out. I remember a time when the idea of a three-way would make my head nearly explode with excitement, but after working in the porn and escorting industries and having more three-ways than I could count, I can honestly say I don't like them. Being with more than one person felt like some kind of sport where you were constantly going back and forth between partners, sucking dicks, getting fucked by one guy to be passed off to another, to have the one guy who was just fucking you go around to your mouth, and force you to choke on his dick while the other guy is fucking you from behind. There were limbs everywhere, someone usually always ended up feeling left out, and it completely destroyed any idea of intimacy for me. Occasionally I would still take part in a three-way and have fun, but for the most part it wasn't something I sought out or loved doing. Jerking off to porn with three or more guys was enjoyable, but once I started escorting and having sex on camera, my tastes changed. Sometimes sex wasn't so interesting, and I began to think of it as work, and sometimes my tastes were pretty "vanilla." But I knew I wasn't spending my time at Dale and Roberto's for my own enjoyment, so it was back to work and focusing on them.

Dale and I began to get into it, and he decided he wanted to fuck me, so he grabbed a condom and I grabbed the lube. After I had greased up my hole, he slid his dick in. We went at it for a while, and I tried to suck Roberto's dick as I was getting fucked, but it was hard to stomach his cock when I was looking at a giant patch of razor burn right in front of my eyes. Behind me, Dale was going at it, and I could feel sweat drip down and trickle onto me. He seemed to be getting in a workout, and I could tell he was getting tired.

"Fuck, I need to stop. It's so hot in here. What temperature did you turn the air conditioner to, Roberto?"

"What?" Roberto snapped.

"What is the temperature in here? It's so fucking hot!"

"I don't know. What did you turn it to, Dale?"

"Let me check."

Dale seemed exasperated with Roberto, and Roberto was obviously annoyed with Dale. I sat there in silence, trying to sneak peeks at the clock whenever possible, praying the time would be up so I could leave this mansion of awkwardness and go back to my hotel.

Roberto turned to me and said, "Listen, I'm just going to try to make him cum as quickly as possible so we can do our own thing. Okay?"

"Sure, yeah... that's fine." I paused for a second and thought to myself, "Did he really just say that?" It was like being out with friends and having that one couple there who absolutely despises each other, and every time they get into a "discussion" an awkward silence falls on the group and you couldn't even cut the tension with a machete.

Dale came back into the room and Roberto—who I now began to see as being bipolar—said to him in the sweetest tone possible, "Hey, babe, I really want you to fuck me. Will you?"

"Uh, sure. Yeah."

Dale lubed up his dick and stuck it into Roberto's ass doggy-style. Roberto was facing me in between my legs, and he began to moan and act like he really enjoyed getting fucked by his lover. Dale started to fuck him faster, and Roberto was bouncing on his dick, moaning as he continued his Oscar-winning performance as a young man who doesn't hate his older boyfriend. Roberto looked up at me, smiled, rolled his eyes, and gave me a look as if to say, *Jesus, Dale ... hurry up, old man, and cum already.* This was all very bizarre to me as I watched this crazy dysfunctional dynamic unfold in front of me.

Dale eventually came, and Roberto rolled his eyes and gave me a look that said, *FINALLY.* He told Dale how great that was and how good it felt. Dale was pleased with his performance and collapsed onto the bed.

Roberto was ready for me to pound him, but I know after everything I saw and the internal dialogue going through my head, there is no way it's going to happen. I made an attempt for the next few minutes to get hard but finally give up. If it's not going to happen, it's not going to happen, and I apologized to them. I felt like a failure, and I was hoping at least Roberto could cum and that might make up for my inability to get it up.

He told me he can't cum because he was hoping to do so as I was fucking him, but he said it was fine. He didn't seem pissed off or anything, just a little annoyed. At this point, I didn't care how he felt. I needed to get the hell out of there, and be on my own.

Dale showed me the bathroom and set up a hot shower for me. I scrubbed myself clean and applied an extra lather of soap all over my body to rid me of the dysfunctional energy I had felt during the past hour. I toweled myself dry and went back to the bedroom to get dressed.

Roberto was waiting for me, and I smiled at him as entered the room. I wasn't sure if I should address what had just happened, but the awkwardness and tension I had felt during the past hour was bothering me, so I decided to ask him about it.

"So is everything okay, or did I walk into something going on between you two?"

"Not really, no... well, we've been fighting for the past few months, and this was kind of our make-up sex."

You've been fighting for the past few months, so you decide to hire an escort to make up? Not only that, but the entire time during your "make-up sex," you bicker, argue, and bitch at each other? Maybe I was not seeing the whole picture here, but this situation spelled all kinds of dysfunction I couldn't begin to wrap my head around. I didn't question him about it further; instead, I apologized for my inability to perform, though he didn't seem bothered by it at all.

"How much do we owe you?" Roberto asked.

"It's five hundred," I said, forgetting the price I had already told Dale earlier.

"Dale said you told him four hundred."

"Shit, sorry... I did. I'm sorry, I forgot. I usually do five hundred dollars for two people for one hour, but I made a mistake and said four hundred earlier."

"No problem," he said and handed me the money.

"So what do you do out here?" I asked.

"I basically hire out all the dancers for some clubs here in L.A. and some in Long Beach. I'm in charge of the go-go boys."

It all made sense now. I generally found people who worked in the club scene really did think they were big deals and elevated themselves to celebrity status. I totally understood now why this kid walked around like his shit didn't stink, and it answered some other questions in my mind as to why it appeared he treated his boyfriend like shit.

"Oh, that's cool," I said.

He asked me about my porn career, though at that time I had only done three scenes. I told him where he could find them, and he said he would look for them later when he jerked off. Roberto was beginning to confuse me, because while he had at first come across as snarky and bitchy, he seemed genuinely interested in my work and seemed to like me. I didn't know how to make sense of it but ultimately I didn't care. I collected my stuff, said my good-byes, and headed back to Long Beach, exhausted.

Later that evening, Roberto sent me some texts asking me about my porn and where he could find me. This was definitely sending me mixed signals. Was he forgiving me for my poor performance? Did he not care? I wasn't sure. All I knew was I had no interest in seeing him again in the future.

A few weeks later, a review on a popular escorting website was posted about me by Roberto. He said he had been disappointed in my ability to get it up, that I had tried to cheat him out of a hundred dollars, and that I should have offered a discount because I could not perform what I had come there to do. I was left feeling speechless and hurt. Could I get it up? Barely. Did I try to rip him off of a hundred dollars? I have never tried to rip off anyone. In fact, I will generally go out of my way to be accommodating to people and their financial situations—within reason—and that comment made me feel like he was accusing me of being dishonest and underhanded. Should I have offered him a discount because I couldn't do what I had come there to do? No. We weren't haggling over knock-off handbags, and he was clearly not the one paying for the time the three of us had spent together, so why was it his concern? I'm not sure. But I guess when you give a West Hollywood queen a little bit of power, they'll think they run the town.

I was more disappointed in myself, because regardless of what I'm doing, I aim to do my best. I struggled for a few weeks after the post was written as to whether or not to respond to the review, because a couple clients and fellow escorts started asking me about the experience and what happened. I kind of wanted to clear my name but decided to let it go. What's done is done. To my surprise, Roberto texted me two months later to tell me he was in Las Vegas, alone this time, and wanted to see me again. Part of me wanted to call him up and scream at him for giving me the negative review, but I figured there was no point. I decided to change my ad and just list myself as a bottom to avoid showing up and disappointing anyone else. This experience also forced me to listen to my inner voice when dealing with clients. If something doesn't feel right, then get the hell out. Times may be tough, but I don't need money so bad that I have to deal with people and situations I'm not one hundred percent comfortable with.

Chapter Thirteen

Conclusion

I have no shame in doing what I do, yet it is difficult to formulate into a sentence what I do for a living when people ask me what I do for work. I have no clue whether or not I should say escort, hooker, or porn star, when in reality my job title is more along the lines of secretary, event planning, therapist, good listener, friend, and dinner date.

I'm not going to lie and say my job is solely to meet clients, go on dinner dates, be arm candy, and leave at the end of the night with an extra five hundred to a thousand dollars in my pocket. Things like that have happened, but they were few and far between. Someone asked me the other day if meeting a client meant I had to sleep with him, and I gave him a puzzled and confused look because I couldn't tell if he was serious. I laughed a bit and told him there was always some kind of expectation of sexual activity. Yes, the client is paying for our time, but there is an expectation, and it is our job to listen to the client's needs and fulfill them as best as possible.

There are many misconceptions about what we as escorts do and the kind of people we are, which is why I wanted to write this book. I believe you attract what you put out there, and I can honestly say I have met a great number of people in my life doing what I am doing now, although there are a lot of people in this industry who I wouldn't trust.

As an escort, I don't spend my nights on the street corner, I don't haggle with Johns about what I will and won't do for money, I don't use meth, crack, or heroin, and I'm not under the control of a pimp. Believe it or not, escorts are businessmen—and -women—and we are out there providing a service that desperately needs to be offered to countless individuals.

Sometimes I question the fact that I am sleeping with married men and I'm helping fulfill sexual fantasies some would label as immoral, disturbing, and wrong, but then I think, Who are we to judge? Sex and sexuality is not black and white, and through escorting and doing porn, I have had to let go of the ideas of what sex is. These values have all been imposed on me by society, my family, the church I grew up with, and the upbringing I had.

The majority of the men I see are married and would label themselves as straight or bisexual. I think many of these men came from a background where it is expected and encouraged to grow up and settle down with a woman. Most get married in their early twenties and have little to no experience dealing with homosexual feelings. Many of the men I have met through escorting don't even start becoming aware of their same-sex feelings until after they are married or well into their twenties, thirties, or possibly later. I've had numerous men contact me who were in their fifties, sixties, and seventies who have suddenly had a desire to explore the same-sex feelings they have been wrestling with for years. In my mind, the first question is, "What took you so long to figure this out?"

I basically knew I was gay since I was about five years old and have been sexually attracted to men my entire life. It baffles me to think of similar men going through their entire lives without acting on these feelings or not even knowing they were gay. I believe the men who had an inkling they were gay got so fed up after years of repressing that part of themselves, they finally got to a place where they could say fuck it and give me—or a fellow escort—a call. Is it ideal for a man to cheat on his wife? No, but it is the reality in which we live. I have an idea of what it feels like to go through your life hiding who you truly are, unable to express it. Sexuality, like relationships, is not black and white. It brings me joy to be able to offer some help and release to these men who are questioning their sexuality and trying to figure out who they are.

What I offer is comfort, companionship, intimacy, and release. We are constantly being told of what is right, what is wrong, what is acceptable, and what is not. I think it's time to say fuck it and start listening to our hearts. What is it I'm trying to tell you? In my thirty-plus years on this planet, I have learned the heart never lies, and everything you need to know is already inside you.

While, yes, I did start working as an escort to make money, travel, and gain new experiences, that was not enough to sustain me in this industry for this period of time. There are days when I want to scream at potential clients for giving me the runaround, lying to me, and blowing me off, but then I realize it's all a part of the game. I have met more good people doing this line of work than bad, and the experiences I have had doing so are invaluable to me. Clients have become friends, mentors, and family. Some have even become closer to me than my actual family because we share a special bond nobody else would understand. I have some clients whose families have rejected them because of who they are, and some clients who have unhealthy, damaging relationships with their spouses. They are unhappy people and they are desperately looking for an escape from their misery. I am happy to be there to give them this experience and provide them with an escape, even if it is temporary.

As far as longevity in this industry, I will continue to do it as long as it feels right. Like anything in life, everything has its season, and when this season comes to an end, my heart will tell me it's time to move on. I'm a hypochondriac and a chronic worrier, and I constantly worry that someday something will happen to me where I cannot continue to escort. I hate living with this kind of fear, but it has helped push me to constantly be on the lookout and prepare myself for the next step and adventure in my life.

I know some men who have been escorting for more than fifteen years and they still look and feel great. They started in the industry as a young boyish twink, and they are now big-muscled daddies who continue to fulfill fantasies for countless men around the world. I also know some men who do this line of work for a few years, see thousands of dollars pass through their hands every week, and have nothing to show for it when they decided to leave the industry. A lot of people leave the escorting business because they're pressured to do so by someone they are dating, or they cannot handle the stress and get tired of the bullshit of dealing with countless individuals and their various quirks and needs. Many escorts come back into the business bitter and jaded because they've realized it's all they know and all they can do where they will make this much money with little to no education and without having to work very hard if they don't want to.

I have many clients who have been hiring escorts for ten, fifteen, and even more than twenty years. Many of them find it much easier than dating or looking for guys at the bar or online. They feel like if they have the funds, they'd rather find someone they're attracted to, spend an hour or so together, pay them their money, and say good-bye. It's a lot less complicated than relationships, and both parties get what they want. A lot of these men who have been hiring for years will tell me to be smart with my money and not fall into the same path they've seen other workers in the sex industry fall into. It's common to see many of these men in the industry escort and do porn for years and get wrapped up in the lifestyle of drugs, frivolous spending, constant money and presents coming in, and someone to always take care of you. The smart ones know it won't last forever and prepare for the time when it will come to an end.

I've had many clients warn me to avoid turning out like so many escorts: addicted to drugs, washed up, out of shape, still hoping for that phone to ring, lowering their hourly rates to embarrassing amounts. It seems like many men have never heard the term "bow out gracefully," and I know this is not something I want for myself. I continue to work on taking care of myself mentally and physically so I do not end up worn out, exhausted, and hating life. No matter how much money you make as an escort—or any profession, really—if you're not happy doing what you are doing and with where you are at in life, then what's the point of doing it?

A big part of me continues to tell myself what I am doing is simply "business." I am running a business, Christopher Daniels is a brand, and I have a website, a Facebook page, and a Twitter account. I reply to e-mails in a timely manner and try to conduct myself professionally at all times. Escorting is a business, and I am a businessman.

Okay, that's true, but I guess there is more to it. Why else am I doing this? For me, a big part of doing this and porn is for the constant approval. Hearing how beautiful you are on a daily basis becomes addictive. You get used to being desired by others, and the attention is nice. Being in porn and escorting is highly narcissistic, and I am fully aware of my overly inflated ego and pure unadulterated narcissism. Part of that is what sustains me in this industry and keeps me going. I can say it's not necessarily a healthy thing, but it is what it is and I recognize it. A lot of escorts and porn stars are highly self-absorbed and are sensitive people. We are put on display for everyone to judge and criticize. Many of us put on a brave face and a "fuck you" attitude, but once you break through the hard exterior, you'll find that many of us are hurt, wounded individuals who desperately want to be loved and accepted. Can I say we honestly get that acceptance and love from escorting? Probably not, but we continue doing it. The money, recognition, and temporary acceptance give us a high and make us feel powerful. How close am I to leaving this business? Who knows? It depends on the day, I guess, but I still keep pushing ahead because it really isn't all that bad of a life. Sure, it's dysfunctional and can bring up some deep-rooted dark feelings I didn't know existed, but I find the good usually outweighs the bad.

In putting together this book, I felt very focused on getting my point across that an escort is a businessman. We are there to make money, and it's the main reason for doing this. In collecting my stories and having to bring up situations from the past few years, I have begun to see the men's reason for coming to us is because they desire some human connection that is not being met in their lives. Something is missing within themselves, and by reaching out to me and other escorts, they are trying to amend that. It's not always about sex. While sex is generally expected during our time together, oftentimes it is not the sole purpose of the meeting and, in fact, sometimes doesn't even happen. I have spent countless hours talking to men, holding them, hearing them talk about everything, from the most trivial bullshit to some of their deepest and darkest feelings. More often than not, the client wants lighthearted conversation and companionship with another man because that's what missing from his live.

While I cannot speak on behalf of escorts everywhere, I know this is a deep-rooted need within myself as well; I am seeking the same from a client, in a sense. We both want love, approval, acceptance, companionship, and intimacy. Getting it from a client isn't exactly necessary for escorts, but it seems to happen at different times. Are we really that much different from each other? Not really. While I wish I could say it was all about business and money, for me it's not. The journey of writing this book has been an up and down experience. Once

I stopped using the left side of my brain when putting my experiences down on paper, I was able to see what escorting was to me: a deep human connection and a need to be close to another person. Not just from the client, but for the escort as well.

5668694R00105

Printed in Great Britain
by Amazon.co.uk, Ltd.,
Marston Gate.